hard up
and **hungry**

hassle free recipes for students,
by students

Betsy Bell

EBURY
PRESS

Special thanks to:

Marcus, Glyn and Richard – for their quirky imagination and capturing the spirit of the book.
Charlotte – for her friendship and alliterations.
Justin & Bobby – for reining in my linguistic excesses and generally defending the English language.
Students – Amelia, Clemmy, Kitty, Laura, Erin, India, Tom, Richard, Henry, David, plus V.J., D.T., Graham and his bull – for all being great posers.
David and Hugo – for saving my computer (and me) from certain meltdown.
And finally Bobby – for more or less saving the day.

This edition published by Ebury Press, 2005
Originally published in 2002 by Penyghent Publishing

1 3 5 7 9 10 8 6 4 2

Text © Betsy Bell 2002, 2005
Photographs © Glyn Howells, Marcus Dawes and Richard Hudson

Betsy Bell has asserted her right to be identified as the author of this work under the Copyright, Designs and Patents Act 1988.

Published by Ebury Press,
Random House, 20 Vauxhall Bridge Road, London SW1V 2SA

Random House Australia (Pty) Limited
20 Alfred Street, Milsons Point, Sydney, New South Wales 2061, Australia

Random House New Zealand Limited
18 Poland Road, Glenfield, Auckland 10, New Zealand

Random House South Africa (Pty) Limited
Enulini, 5A Jubilee Road, Parktown 2193, South Africa

The Random House Group Limited Reg. No. 954009

www.randomhouse.co.uk

A CIP catalogue for this book is available from the British Library

Edited by: Justin Whiteley
Cover Photography by: Richard Hudson
Inside Photography by: Glynn Howells and Marcus Dawes

ISBN 0-09190489-7

Printed and bound in China

Contents

Glossary

Baste   Spoon sauce, butter or liquid over food during cooking.

Beat   Mix food thoroughly and with vigour, using a spoon or whisk.

Blanch   Throw vegetables into boiling water, bring back to the boil, then drain. This retains fresh greenness in certain veg, and removes strong and undesired flavours.

Boil   An eruption of water or liquid, sending up loads of really enthusiastic bubbles.

Brown   To seal juices into meat by quickly sautéing it on all sides over a high temp.

Chop   Cut food into small pieces, or finely chop into very small pieces.

Garnish   Here, a garnish doesn't mean a nattily-placed piece of parsley, but a secondary ingredient to be used in addition to a recipe, like baked eggs with a garnish of sautéed mushroom.

Fold   Gently incorporate an ingredient, with minimum disruption.

Infuse   Flavour a liquid with herbs, spices or garlic.

Poach   Submerge food and cook in liquid that is barely simmering, smoked haddock for example.

Ramekin   A round heatproof ceramic pot, measuring about 8cm across and 5cm deep.

Sauté   Cook food at a fairly high temp in some form of fat.

Sift   Shake dry ingredients through a sieve to lighten, and remove lumps.

Season   Add salt and pepper to taste.

Simmer   Cook food in liquid at a very slow boil. Only extremely subdued bubbles should be detected.

Sweat   Cook chopped veg in some form of fat over a medium/low heat.

Introduction

It was only when my two strapping lads left home to tackle life and college that I realised how little they (and most of their friends) knew about culinary survival.

The first two months at college were just dandy; pizzas were consumed in endless Huts and Expresses; burgers in bars and Kings. On nights in, pre-cooked meals were expertly removed from sleeves, pierced and microwaved.

Motherly offers to deliver rich, filling broths from North Yorkshire were scoffed at. That is until funds intended to last six months were running out before the third month had even begun.

With a dwindling cash flow and absolutely no knowledge of cooking or shopping, the boys had become borderline unhealthy, totally hard up and extremely hungry.

The moral of this story is that eating out, even at simple pizza places, is expensive and not very healthy. The same is true of pre-cooked meals.

Panic not. With a little forward planning, sensible shopping and a few foolproof recipes under your belt you can escape the bank manager and malnutrition, and still have time to play.

Essential Top Tips

Pool your resources

If you share digs with friends, think about having a weekly collection for food. After all, £120 per week buys a lot more groceries for four people than £30 for one. It will also save you worrying about whose buns you're buttering.

Plan ahead

Make a plan of your weekly menu. I know this sounds ridiculously housewife-ish and geeky, and sure, life is always changing, but by and large it works. Here's why:

A plan focuses your shopping. If you shop at random, half the supermarket will end up in your trolley, you will spend a small fortune and when you arrive home, you will probably still wonder what there is for dinner. So make a list.

Having a menu plan will help you organise your cooking. For example, you can use your oven to cook two dishes in one go; use leftovers in other recipes; use the same ingredients several times, thus reducing your shopping list and enabling you to buy in bulk.

You can buy the majority of your ingredients for a week or two in one supermarket mega shop. This will save you both time and money. You can't fault that.

Shop sensibly

Nipping round to your local convenience store will have the bank manager (and doctor) banging at your door in no time. The same is true of takeaways or any pre-prepared meal.

Try your best to cook healthy food at home and buy the bulk of your ingredients at supermarkets, local butchers, greengrocers and street markets (brilliant for fresh veggies and fish).

Keep a store cupboard

Have a good supply of dry goods and non-perishables on hand. This will ensure that on even the busiest and leanest of days you can still pull together a meal.

Read the recipe through

Feel comfortable with it before embarking on its final preparation. Don't be put off a dish if you haven't got all the ingredients. A recipe is a guide, not food fascism.

Make cooking fun

This is really the most important Top Tip I can give you. Cooking delicious, healthy food does not have to be scary. Make friends with a few recipes. Once you've tested them out a couple of times you might even enjoy cooking them.

Try taking turns to cook with flatmates or, better still, all join in together. I don't believe what they say about too many chefs spoiling the broth. I've had some good laughs cooking with friends.

Eating is something we all have to do everyday. Try to see cooking not as an effort and a drag, but as a pleasant and essential part of daily life.

It can be fun, I promise.

Weights, Measures & Symbols

These symbols are used as a guide at the top of every recipe.

⌘   = Top burner only
V   = Vegetarian dishes
SC   = Store cupboard ingredients only
£X   = A rough cost **per person:** £1 is up to £1, £2 up to £2, and so on

While you are still finding your culinary feet you may feel more comfortable following each recipe to the gram. But with the exception of baked goods, precise measurements aren't really necessary. You can, in fact, be quite free-range in your approach to cooking.

Here are some measures and their rough equivalents:

Butter

250g is approx 1 cup* or 16 tbs
150g is approx 1/2 cup or 8 tbs
25g is just under 2 tbs

Cheese

250g is 2¹/₂ cups or 650ml
200g is 2 cups or 500ml
150g is 1¹/₂ cups or 375ml
100g is 1 cup or 250ml
50g is ¹/₂ cup or 150ml

Sugar

200g is 1 cup or 16 tbs
150g is ³/₄ cup or 12 tbs
100g is ¹/₂ cup or 8 tbs
50g is ¹/₄ cup or 4 tbs

Flour

200g is 1¹/₃ cups or 22 tbs
150g is 1 cup or 16 tbs
100g is ²/₃ cup or 11 tbs
50g is ¹/₃ cup or 5 tbs

*1 cup equals an average tea mug or 250ml.

TOP TIPS:

- The recipes in this book are mostly for 4 people. If you are cooking for two simply halve the amounts, or enjoy the glory of leftovers.

- Ovens are volatile creatures. Their temps can experience mood swings according to the number of dishes they're cooking, as well as their time of life. In student digs this is especially true. Take this into account when timing a recipe. Always check food for doneness rather than relying on precise timings.

Store Cupboard

It's vital to have a good stash of herbs, tins, dry goods and non-perishables on hand. Not only will many of these things be part of a recipe but with a little imagination they can be pulled together to create a simple supper on their own.

Tins and Jars
Anchovies
Corned beef
Red wine vinegar
Tomato ketchup and purée
Pesto sauce
Sun dried tomatoes
Jalapeno peppers
Soy sauce and Thai fish sauce
Hoi sin sauce
Tuna fish
Olive oil and vegetable oil
Olives: black and green*
Tinned plum tomatoes
Mayonnaise
Mustard
Jam and honey
Capers

Dried Things
Dried chilli flakes
Salt and pepper
Dried thyme
Dried rosemary
Cumin
Coriander seeds
Fennel seeds
Cardamom pods
Cayenne pepper
Coffee

Tea bags
Sugar
Flour
Stock powder or cubes
Basmati rice
Arborio rice
Long grain rice
Couscous
Dried pasta of choice
Fine Chinese noodles
Cannellini beans, tinned
Kidney beans, tinned
Chickpeas, tinned
Puy lentils, dried
Brown lentils, dried

Potatoes
Onions
Garlic

Fridge +
Long life milk
Butter
Fresh ginger root
Cheese: Parmesan, Cheddar, Feta
Eggs
Bacon and/or pancetta cubes
Vacuum packed gammon joint

*Avoid pre-pitted olives. They can be tasteless and more expensive than their stoned cousins. Use Kalamatas. Liven them up by adding a few chillies or herbs to the jar.
+ These will keep for up to one month or longer in a fridge if unopened. Once opened Cheddar and Parmesan will generally last 2 weeks if wrapped in cling film or greaseproof paper. Feta will only last for 5 to 6 days, and pig bits 5 days once released from their vacuum packing, but again they must be properly wrapped up or cooked. Eggs generally last 2 weeks.

Equipment

Obviously all your living conditions vary. But let's face it, none of you will be blessed with a gleaming state-of-the-art kitchen, proudly boasting a full gas range, food processor, blender, acres of counter and storage space and a cavernous deep freeze.

The reality is that most of you will have to cope with the barest of necessities in the tiniest of kitchens.

Halls of residence vary from college to college but in general they tend to have a top burner, a microwave and an electric kettle. In some cases there is the ultimate luxury of a dolls' house-sized refrigerator.

Most student/young person-oriented flats and houses come equipped with a refrigerator/freezer, a cooker, an electric kettle, toaster and, in most cases, a microwave.

Pots and pans are trickier to predict. If they are very old and nasty or if there is even the slightest trace of irremovable matter my advice would be to invest in one or two pots and pans of your own. Or better yet, borrow some from home.

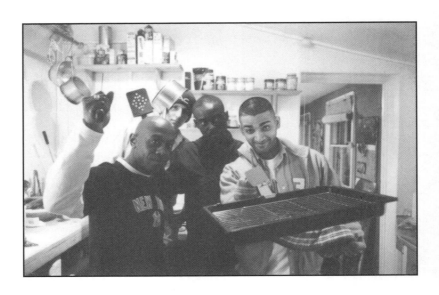

Utensils

Here is the essential 'survival kit' of utensils. The cost need not be too alarming and if lovingly kept they should last the course.

None of my recipes requires the use of expensive and space-consuming gadgets.

Preparation

Chopping knife (very sharp)
Paring knife
Wooden spoon
Potato peeler
Slotted spoon
Scissors
Potato masher
Balloon whisk
Spatula
Small plastic chopping board
Tin opener
Cheese grater
Measuring spoons
Measuring jug: Stewart's dry and liquid.*
Sieve
Colander
Cling film, tin foil, freezer bags

Pots & pans

2 roasting tins, 35 x 26cms, ish
1 or 2 small saucepans
1 large saucepan
Frying pan 25cms, ish
Round or oval baking dish 25 x 20cms, ish
2 mixing bowls
4 ramekins, handy but optional

*This is the jewel in the crown of kitchen utensils. It measures liquids and dry goods in both metric and imperial.

Shopping

Acquiring sensible shopping skills is a key factor in your quest for civilized survival. Shopping at the neighbourhood convenience shop or deli every day can quickly eat a hole in your pocket.

Provided you have an adequate amount of storage space try to do a weekly or even fortnightly supermarket mega shop. Top this up with fresh meat, fruit and veg from your nearest street market or butcher.

For those of you living in Halls or with very little storage space, keep as good a store cupboard as possible (use sacking boxes and hanging baskets) then buy enough fresh food for, say, 2 or 3 days.

Supermarkets

Apart from your local street market, supermarkets really are the best value for money. You can also do your entire shopping under one roof, which is a definite time saver.

The biggest drawback in buying a week/fortnight's worth of food and drink is the transportation. Supermarkets are very often located in areas which are inconvenient to get to and, more importantly, from.

There are more 'Local' and 'Central' mini supermarkets mushrooming in town centres but you still don't want to hump a full week's worth of food and drink home in a backpack.

Don' panic. Being young, you will probably know how to drive a computer. All the major supermarkets now offer on-line shopping and home delivery. This service could set you back a fiver but there are real advantages:

• Food is delivered straight to your door, no transport hassle.

• Shopping on-line concentrates the mind on what is really needed, reducing the temptation to go on a greed-induced shopping spree.

• You can schedule the delivery for a time that suits you.

There is one downside to shopping on-line. Sometimes fruit and veg is not as fresh as you would have chosen for yourself.

The way around this is to buy most of your fresh produce on an as-you-need-it basis from street markets, or indeed a convenient supermarket.

For those of you without a computer or access to one (is there such a person? If so, ring me, I love you), I suggest you make friends with someone who has a car or big muscles.

But, seriously, your best bet is to stock up the store cupboard when an opportunity arises, then buy fresh food every three days or so. If you are sharing a flat with friends make a weekly menu plan (there are some suggestions later in the book) and take the fresh food buying in turns. Alternatively, use a minicab for your return journey. Most shops have a direct line to cab companies by the front door. A minicab should cost no more than a home delivery.

TOP TIPS:

- Have a list of what you actually need. Never shop at random or you will spend far more than intended.

- Try not to shop when you are hungry.

- Most supermarkets have 'value' and 'own' brands that really are worth buying.

- You can pick up some great bargains on food that is about to go past its sell by date. I have bought food for half-price on the date by which it was due to be sold. Provided you eat it within a day or two, you will live to tell the tale.

- Beware of buying food that is made to be convenient. The more that has been done to pre-prepare the food, the more you will pay.

Street Markets

I adore street markets. They sell food that is great value, generally fresh (do always inspect carefully) and towards the end of the day on 'Sale'.

Street markets tend to be intimate in a matey sort of way. When I was cooking in London some of my best relationships were with the purveyors of fresh vegetables and exotic herbs in the Northcote Road and Portobello Road markets.

There are markets scattered throughout Britain's cities and county towns, which also boast loads of fruit and veg stands offering amazing bargains. If there isn't one near your place of work, rest or play I will eat my hat.

Wet fish is always a good buy at the street market. Make friends with the fishmonger as you don't want to be doing all that boning by yourself.

Butchers

If you have access to a deep freeze you can buy all your meat and poultry for the week/fortnight during your supermarket mega shop. If not, you will either have to resort to vegetarian mid-week, return to the supermarket or find a convenient and reliable butcher.

It's important to develop a congenial working relationship with your butcher. He can guide you towards good buys and hopefully do some of the fiddly trimming and chopping for you.

Do always ask how long the meat has been in the shop and by when it should be eaten. Unlike meat bought at the supermarket, butcher's meat does not come with a sell-by date stamped on the front.

Compare the prices between the butcher and the supermarket. Some butchers can be very pricey, depending on their location and reputation.

Storage

Having gone to all the trouble of buying your food it now makes sense to store it properly. This not only helps fresh food and leftovers last longer but reduces the possibility of food poisoning.

If you are sharing a flat or house with a few mates you will probably not have a huge problem with storage and/or thieving hands. Halls of residence, which can sometimes accommodate as many as 12 greedy souls per kitchen, pose more of a problem.

Freezers

TOP TIPS:

- If you have the benefit of a biggish freezer you are well ahead in the game.

- Buy enough meat, poultry, bread and other freezer-friendly perishables for the whole week, or even two, in a big shop-up. You can freeze these foods until needed, eliminating the need to shop much more during the week.

- Remember to put frozen food straight in the freezer once you get home from the shops.

- Make sauces, soups and stews in quantity and store batches in the freezer.

- Always label and date items destined for the deep freeze. What looks perfectly obvious raw can suddenly become totally unrecognisable once frozen. Try to resist the temptation to hoard. You never know what you might find lurking in your freezer after months of neglect.

- Use old plastic water bottles or margarine tubs to freeze soups and sauces.

- You can freeze orange juice, sliced bread, bagels, muffins and bacon. This avoids an early morning panic on the breakfast front. These items can all be cooked or microwaved from frozen.

Fridges

TOP TIPS:

- To avoid truly ugly matter growing in the fridge, try wiping down the inside with a shot of kitchen spray from time to time.

- Keep fresh food such as meat, cheese, butter, yoghurt and all leftovers covered up with cling film or waxed paper. This is just good hygiene. Pure and simple. Food left uncovered will also dry up and smell out the refrigerator. Don't store leftovers in opened tins. Decant into a mug or bowl.

- Release meat and poultry from its plastic packaging and rewrap using greaseproof paper. This prevents the food from 'sweating' and going off. Do make a note of its sell by date.

- Do a monthly sell-by swoop. If in doubt, throw it out.

- If you share your fridge with the hoards in Halls you are likely to 'lose' your tastiest morsels. Think about keeping your fresh food in a plastic storage box labelled with your name and possibly a chain and padlock…

Store Cupboards

- Metal or plastic three-layer hanging baskets make wonderful storage units. You can hook them up in all sorts of nooks and crannies and they save precious counter space.

- Children's plastic stacking boxes also make great storage containers. These are particularly useful if you're living in Halls. Safely stored in your room, you can easily transport your store cupboard food to the kitchen and be sure it will still be there when you need it.

- Check out boxes that come with airtight lids. They are useful for keeping hungry rodents at bay.

- Glass canisters are pretty to look at and if you have loads of counter space they make excellent receptacles for tea, flour, sugar, pasta, pulses and basically anything that tends to spill out everywhere once opened.

- If your kitchen and pocket don't stretch to these arty items you may well consider using plastic tupperware-style containers. Don't laugh, they're brilliant. These natty little receptacles keep things fresh and dust free for ages and come in every conceivable shape and size. Plastic 'clips' are also useful for keeping rice, pasta, cereal and so on under control once opened. If all else fails there is always sticky tape.

- Don't forget to check for freshness from time to time. Even store cupboard items have a finite life span.

Storing fruit

In the interest of freshness, the more you can store in the fridge the better. Having said this, certain fruits must be left out to ripen.

Fruit eaten at room temperature tastes much better. If you can be bothered to think about it, a rotation between the fridge and fruit bowl works a treat. Try storing the bulk of your fruit in the fridge then transplanting 2 days worth into an attractive fruit bowl, ready for munching.

If you're pushed for fridge space try creating a makeshift larder on your window-sill. Being Britain, your fruit will stay nice and cool all year round.

The best solution for everyone is to find a convenient street seller, or greengrocer, and buy your fruit as and when you need it.

TOP TIPS:

*   If you want to speed up the ripening process, try placing your fruit in a paper bag with a banana. It's quirky but true. Beware: once ripeness has been achieved you had better eat up, or of course, chill.

*   Don't chill bananas. Try to hang them from something so they ripen evenly without developing brown patches. Use old bananas for muffins and smoothies.

Storing veg

Almost all vegetables last longer if chilled. If you have the space, I would recommend you refrigerate as much as possible. Alternatively, try to find a cool corner to store any veg that has not sought shelter in the fridge.

Certain veggies are okay left out of the fridge (maybe in the hanging basket): tomatoes are best not chilled. Onions, garlic, carrots and other root vegetables are quite happy non-chilled. Potatoes last longer if kept in the dark in a bag.

Soups

Soup works wonders at filling the stomach and soothing the soul. There can be little to beat a steaming bowl of homemade soup after a long, hard day or night.

All these soups are more or less meals in themselves, and most are suitable for vegetarians.

None of the recipes needs a food processor.

TOP TIPS:

•   If you don't happen to have a vast supply of homemade chicken stock lurking in your fridge, try using Marigold Swiss Vegetable Bouillon Powder or Knorr stock cubes instead. Stock cubes are full of salt so be aware of this when you are adding your seasoning.

•   Homemade soup costs a fraction of its store-bought cousin. Consider investing in a thermos and taking some soup into college or work for an inexpensive and healthy lunch.

•   Soup can be made in bulk and kept, covered, in the fridge for 4 or 5 days. If you have a deep freeze, soup can be frozen in sandwich bags or plastic water bottles with their tops cut off.

Leek and Potato Soup

Serves 4
⌘ V £1

4 leeks, whites only, finely sliced
3 potatoes, peeled and cut into 3cm cubes
1 1/2 litres vegetable stock
1 tbs olive oil
25g butter

- Melt the butter in a medium/large saucepan along with the oil.

- Add the chopped potatoes and leeks and sweat for 5 minutes, stirring to avoid browning.

- Pour in the stock and bring the whole lot to the boil. Reduce the heat so that the soup is cooking at a gentle simmer and cover.

- Test the potatoes for tenderness (poke them with a fork or knife) after about 10 minutes. When the potatoes are soft, remove the soup from the heat and season with salt and freshly ground pepper.

- You can mash the potatoes up a bit with a masher or leave as hunky numbers.

  TOP TIP: A little cream stirred into this soup never goes amiss.

Oriental Noodle Soup

Serves 4
⌘ £2

2 raw chicken breasts, cut into 2cm cubes
1 tbs ginger, finely chopped
1 tbs soy sauce
1 tbs Thai fish sauce
1/2 tsp sugar
1 tsp dried chilli
1 1/2 litres chicken stock
3 spring onions, finely sliced
125g fine oriental noodles
1/2 small cabbage, very finely chopped
Bunch of fresh coriander
Juice of 1 lime

- Bring the stock to a simmer in a large saucepan.

- Add the ginger, chilli, sauces, sugar and chicken and return to a simmer.

- Cook for 2 minutes then throw in the noodles, cabbage and onions.

- Bring to the boil then cook for 3 minutes. Poke at the noodles; they always need a little loosening up.

- When cooked, squeeze in the lime juice and scatter with torn coriander.

  TOP TIPS: Prepare all the ingredients before you begin cooking. With all oriental recipes there is a scary amount of slicing and chopping, but the cooking itself only takes a matter of minutes. Don't be put off by the amount of prepping – this soup is really worth the effort. Get some friends over for supper and hand them some knives.

  Don't overcook and risk losing the lovely freshness of the vegetables.

Minestrone

Serves 4
⌘ V £1

1 tbs olive oil
1 onion, chopped
2 sticks celery, chopped
2 small, firm courgettes, in 1cm slices
1/2 head of Savoy cabbage, shredded
1 x 400g tin chopped plum tomatoes
1 tbs tomato purée
2 or 3 waxy potatoes, cut into 3cm cubes
2 cloves garlic, finely chopped
1 1/2 litres vegetable stock
Bunch of fresh basil, optional

• Gently sweat the celery, onion and garlic in a medium saucepan with the olive oil.

• After 5 minutes add the tomato purée, tinned tomatoes and potatoes. Cook for another 5 minutes before pouring in the stock.

• Cover, and simmer for 10 minutes or until the potatoes are tender but not mushy. Slice the courgettes into 1cm discs and then cut the discs into quarters.

• Add the courgettes and shredded cabbage to the soup and simmer for 7 minutes. Season, add the basil and serve with a dribble of olive oil and some Parmesan.

Top Tips: To make this soup go even further add a tin of drained cannellini beans along with the courgettes and cabbage.

Committed carnivores can add a few slices of bacon or some left over gammon to the soup. Put the meat in at the beginning, along with the onion and garlic.

Barley Soup

Serves 4
⌘ V £1

175g pearl barley*
2 leeks, whites only, sliced
2 sticks celery, sliced
1 carrot, chopped
1 tbs olive oil
1 onion, chopped
1 1/2 litres veg stock

- Put the oil in a medium/large saucepan and add the prepared vegetables. Gently sweat for 5 minutes without browning.

- Add the barley and stock, cover and simmer for 30 minutes or until the barley is tender.

- Season to taste.

  TOP TIPS: For those of you in search of meat think about adding some bacon or gammon. Pop in your pig of choice along with the veggies. You can more or less throw any old vegetable into this broth.

  * Do be certain to use the no soak variety of barley

Pasta

I love pasta. It's simple to prepare, inexpensive and totally delicious. Pasta is the perfect easy supper after a long day when you've had no time to think about eating. There are seven pasta recipes in this chapter, plus a few made from the store cupboard alone, but nobody really needs a recipe to create marvellous pasta dishes. Experiment with your own ideas and pass them on to your friends, or to me for my next book.

TOP TIPS:

* Buy dried pasta as opposed to mass produced 'fresh'. It is far less expensive and lasts nearly forever as an essential part of your store cupboard. Supermarkets carry their own brands and 'value' pasta.

* Read the labelling carefully and look out for durum wheat semolina pasta. This is what you want to buy.

* Use a large pot to cook pasta as you must give it plenty of room to roam. Remember to stir occasionally.

* Allow 100g of pasta per head.

* Use 1 litre of water per 100g of pasta. Get the water really boiling before adding the pasta. Salt and a tablespoon of olive oil help the pasta to stay slippery and tasty.

* Try not to over cook it. The cooking time will vary according to the size of the pasta. Test a strand about 1 minute short of the recommended cooking time. Perfectly cooked pasta should be al dente, which means it offers some resistance to the bite.

* Make certain the sauce is ready before the pasta. Never leave pasta waiting or it will become cold and sticky. Drain your cooked pasta into a colander or tip the water out of the pot using the lid to hold the pasta back. Serve from a warmed bowl or straight from the cooking pot.

Spaghetti with Fennel and Smoked Bacon

Serves 4

⌘ **£2**

2 bulbs fennel
Juice of 1/2 lemon
200g smoked bacon or pancetta, chopped
400g spaghetti
3 tbs olive oil
Parmesan cheese, grated

- Put a large pot of water on to boil. Add a dash of salt and a spoonful of oil.

- Next put 1 tbs olive oil and bacon in a frying pan and brown. This should take about 5 minutes. A lid would be a good idea at this stage.

- Roughly chop your fennel into slices or chunks, removing the small core in the centre and the feathers at the top.

- Heat the remaining 2 tbs olive oil and the fennel in the frying pan with the bacon. Cook for around 5 minutes or until the fennel is tender but not mushy.

- Squeeze the lemon juice all over the fennel/bacon mixture and season with pepper. Remember the bacon/pancetta will make this dish fairly salty.

- Cook the pasta until it's al dente, drain into a colander, slide into a warm bowl and top with the fennel sauce. Give the whole lot a good sprinkling of Parmesan.

   Top Tip: If not used immediately, fennel will brown once sliced. To avoid this place the sliced fennel in a bowl of water with the juice of one lemon.

Pasta with Capers, Tomatoes, Anchovies and Black Olives

Serves 4
⌘ V SC £1

1 x 50g tin anchovies
2 cloves of garlic, finely chopped
Capers, as many as you like
2 x 400g tins chopped plum tomatoes
Handful black olives
3 tbs olive oil
2 tbs tomato purée
400g pasta of choice

- Pour 3 tbs olive oil into a medium saucepan and add the chopped garlic. Gently cook for a minute. Be carefully not to brown the garlic.

- Add the tinned tomatoes, tomato purée, anchovies, capers and olives and simmer for 20 minutes or until you can't hold back any longer.

- Put a large pot of water on to boil. Add salt and a splash of olive oil.

- Cook your pasta according to the instructions and drain in a colander when ready.

- Top the pasta with lots of hot, pungent sauce. If heat is what you're after, sprinkle with dried chilli flakes.

  TOP TIP: This sauce improves with age. Consider making a double recipe and keeping it in the freezer or fridge for a few days.

Pasta with Bacon, Peas and Cream

Serves 4
⌘ £2

1 x 284g pot of double cream
150g or 1 cup frozen peas
75g butter
180g to 200g smoked bacon, gammon or pancetta cubes
400g pasta of choice
Pinch dried chilli (optional)

- Put a large pot of water on to boil. Add a dash of salt and a spoonful of oil.

- Cut the bacon, gammon or pancetta into pieces and fry (in a little of the butter with a dash of oil if using gammon).

- When the pig of choice looks cooked, add the cream and season with a little salt, pepper and a sprinkle of dried chilli for a bit of excitement.

- Meanwhile cook your pasta in the boiling water. To save on the washing up, throw the peas in with the pasta for the last minute of cooking.

- Drain the pasta and peas in a colander. Place in a warmed serving bowl, or back in the saucepan, and mix with remaining butter and the creamy bacon sauce.

  TOP TIPS: If you are feeling especially greedy and in need of the comfort of dairy produce, give this dish a generous topping of grated cheddar cheese.

  This recipe is an excellent use for leftover gammon.

Spaghetti with Tomato and Basil sauce

Serves 4
⌘ V £1

2 x 400g tins of chopped plum tomatoes
2 cloves garlic, finely chopped
A tiny pinch of sugar
2 tbs olive oil
Bunch of fresh basil, torn
400g spaghetti

- Pour the olive oil in a medium saucepan and add the chopped garlic. Gently cook for 1 minute, being careful not to brown the garlic.

- Expertly open the tins of tomatoes and add them to the garlic along with a pinch of sugar and the basil. Leave to simmer on a low heat for around 20 to 30 minutes. Taste for seasoning. Beware of the erupting sauce covering your kitchen in a fine lava-like spray.

- Around 10 minutes before the sauce is ready drop the pasta into boiling water and cook.

- Test pasta for doneness and then drain if ready.

- Serve in a warmed serving bowl topped with the tomato sauce.

  TOP TIPS: This recipe is even more delicious with fresh mozzarella cheese thrown in. Chop two fresh mozzarella 'balls' into 3cm pieces and add them to the sauce at the very last minute.

  If you are blessed with a deep freeze, double the recipe and freeze the other half, sans cheese, for a later date.

Pasta with Broccoli and Anchovies

Serves 4
⌘ V £1

2 heads broccoli
1 x 50g tin anchovies, cut in half
4 cloves garlic, sliced
4 to 5 tbs olive oil
400g pasta of choice
Parmesan cheese, grated

- Put a large pot of water on to boil.

- Separate your broccoli into individual sections, florettes, and blanch in boiling water.

- Slice the garlic into thin slivers and place in the frying pan with the drained anchovies and olive oil. Cook very gently.

- After 2 minutes, add the broccoli. Cook for a further 2 minutes or until the broccoli is cooked through but still crunchy and bright green.

- Meanwhile some helpful soul should be cooking your pasta in boiling, salted and oiled water. When al dente and drained, add the broccoli mixture. Be generous and serve with a large chunk of grated Parmesan cheese.

Pasta with Spicy Sausage and Spinach

Serves 4
⌘ **£2**

4 tbs olive oil
4 big and spicy sausages
2 cloves garlic, chopped
1 x 400g tin chopped plum tomatoes
30ml red wine, optional
150g to 200g fresh spinach, washed
400g pasta of choice

- Place the sausages in a frying pan with 4 tbs olive oil and fry, breaking the sausage into chunks as you go.

- When the sausages are more or less cooked and disassembled, add the chopped garlic and gently cook for another 2 minutes.

- Add a splash of red wine and allow to cook off (evaporate) for a minute or two.

- Add the tomatoes to the sausage mixture. Let the whole lot simmer away for 10 minutes.

- Add the spinach in batches, pressing it into the sauce and letting it wilt down as you go. When all the spinach is wilted and incorporated into the sauce give it a good stir and season.

- By now your pasta should have been plunged into a violent whirl of boiling water and be well under way. Test for doneness and drain.

- Place pasta in warmed serving bowl or back into the pot and drizzle with remaining oil. Top with the sausage and tomato sauce and get stuck in.

    Top Tip: If you can't find spicy sausages just use ordinary porkers and add a pinch of dried chilli when you break them up.

Spaghetti Bolognese

Serves 4
⌘ **£2**

450g good quality minced beef
4 rashers of bacon, chopped
1 onion, chopped
1 clove garlic, finely minced
1 x 450g tin chopped plum tomatoes
$1/2$ x 142g tin of tomato purée
300ml chicken stock
Pinch of dried oregano
1 tbs flour
400g spaghetti
2 tbs olive oil

- Fry the bacon and minced beef together in a medium saucepan until the meat is brown through. Drain off any excess fat. If the mince is extra lean you may need to add a splash of olive oil.

- Remove the meat from the pan onto a plate. Add the chopped onion, with a slosh of olive oil, to the pan.

- Gently sweat the onion for 4 or 5 minutes then add the garlic.

- Give the onion mixture a good stir and return the mince to the saucepan along with the flour. Give another stir to incorporate the flour then add the tinned tomatoes, tomato purée, chicken stock and oregano.

- Put a lid over the pan and gently simmer for 45 minutes. Taste for seasoning. Stir occasionally to avoid sticking.

- Cook pasta according to instructions, then drain and top with the meat sauce.

    Top Tip: This sauce is an excellent freezer and can also be kept covered in the fridge for 3 days.

Risotto

Risotto is an Italian recipe of short grain rice that, with the addition of hot stock and constant stirring, becomes a delicious, creamy mass of rib-sticking goodness. It is the ultimate comfort food and is cheap and easy to make. Give it a whirl and you'll soon become a master in the art of the perfect risotto.

Rice

Always use either arborio or carnaroli rice. Arborio is the most widely available and has the ability to absorb stock and produce a creamy soupiness while still retaining its firmness. Never rinse the rice before cooking.

Stock

It is important to keep stock hot while adding it to the risotto. Mix up some powdered or cubed stock. You can mix the stock in a heatproof measuring jug using boiling water. If you think it's cooling off too quickly, give it a blast in the microwave.

Pans

An even heat is important when cooking risotto. Try to use a pan with a thick flat bottom.

In the world according to risotto, the three key words are:

- **Sizzle**
  Let your rice become coated in the fat and sauté over high heat for 3 or 4 minutes before adding your wine and stock. Keep the rice moving at all times to avoid burning. If the rice begins to make a sizzling noise, so much the better, as this means it's working.

- **Simmer**
  Keep the rice cooking at a gentle and constant simmer. If you boil it too hard it will be raw and hard on the inside and mushy on the outside. On the other hand, if you cook it too slowly the rice will become gluey and nasty. The ideal risotto should be al dente, firm but tender.

- **Stir**

  Now for the downside. A proper risotto demands your undivided attention. Constant stirring is needed to achieve a delicious sloppy risotto; there is no way around it. Arborio rice should take around 20 minutes to cook, but test for doneness along the way.

Add whatever you fancy

Risotto lends itself to many things. You can eat it plain, with a scratching of Parmesan, or you can add veggies, meats, leftovers, you name it. (See p.38)

Don't hang about

Have warm bowls ready and waiting to receive the risotto straight off the assembly line.

Top Tip: You can eat leftover risotto. Simply place the desired amount in a bowl, cover with cling film and reheat in the microwave. Don't try to reheat in a saucepan as it tends to become sticky and dry.

Any of the following things, and many more, can be added to a basic risotto. Use the recipe on page 39 as the 'key' to all risottos in this book.

- A jar of ready-made pesto (delicious with roast chicken). Add towards the end of cooking.

- Sun dried tomatoes. Chop into quarters and add half way through the cooking process.

- Goats cheese and spinach. Blanch spinach and add towards end of cooking. Crumble cheese on top of the finished risotto.

- Prawns, lemon rind and chopped parsley. Add these at the very end of cooking.

- Saffron and Parma ham. Add the saffron threads to your stock. Drape the ham in shreds over the finished risotto. This is not the cheapest way to eat risotto.

- Fennel, bacon or pancetta, and lemon. Add these at the beginning of cooking along with the onion and garlic.

- Ham and peas. Add 5 minutes before the end of the cooking process.

- Peas and fresh mint. Blanch the peas and add with the chopped mint (say 4 large leaves) during the last 5 minutes of cooking.

Basic Risotto

Serves 4
⌘ V SC £1

300g arborio rice
1 litre veg stock
70g butter
1 tbs olive oil
1 medium onion, finely chopped
2 cloves garlic, chopped
2 sticks celery, finely chopped
30ml white wine, optional
Good scratching of Parmesan

- Heat the stock.

- Set a medium saucepan over medium high heat and put in the oil and half the butter. When the butter melts add the onion, garlic and celery, then gently sweat for 5 minutes or until tender.

- Add the rice to the vegetable mixture, making sure all the grains get a good coating of fat.

- Continue to sauté until the rice is slightly translucent, sizzling and hissing. Keep the rice moving in the pan at all times to avoid browning.

- Add the white wine and cook until absorbed.

- Begin adding your stock, one ladleful at a time. Add a ladle of stock, stir, let the rice absorb the moisture, then add another ladle of stock, stir, and so on.

- When the rice is al dente (after around 20 minutes) remove from the heat. Add the remaining butter and the Parmesan.

  TOP TIP: A dollop of cream or crème fraîche makes this dish even more delicious and creamy.

Risotto with Mushrooms

Serves 4
⌘ V £2

Basic Risotto recipe ingredients (see p.39)
300g mixed mushrooms
Bunch of fresh flat leaf parsley, chopped
Squeeze of lemon
1 tbs olive oil
25g butter

- Chop the mushrooms – slices or chunks are both fine.

- Set a medium saucepan over medium high heat and add the butter and olive oil. Wait a minute for the oil to become hot then throw in your mushrooms (if you feel ambitious, consider cooking your mushrooms in two batches, they sog out less this way).

- Sauté the mushrooms at high heat for 2 minutes, stirring at all times. Season with salt and pepper, parsley and lemon juice. Give them one more stir and decant onto a plate.

- Using the same saucepan, carry on with the Basic Risotto recipe, adding the mushrooms towards the end of the cooking process.

- When ready, serve with a green salad and a lump of fresh Parmesan.

   Top Tips: Don't use button mushrooms in a risotto. They are more or less tasteless and it's easy to do better. Most supermarkets and street markets sell a wide variety of tasty and tempting mushrooms. If you're feeling poor buy flat field, brown cap, portobello, shitake and oyster. Otherwise, girolle, dried cep and chanterelle are aromatic and delicious.

   Never wash mushrooms in water. They are like little sponges and will become disgustingly soggy. Instead, try peeling off their outer layer or gently brushing them with a pastry brush or tea towel.

Risotto of Courgettes, Rosemary and Thyme

Serves 4
⌘ V £1

Basic Risotto recipe ingredients (see p.39)
3 small, firm courgettes
Pinch of dried rosemary
Pinch of dried thyme

* Make sure you use firm and smallish courgettes for this dish. The older and larger ones tend to lose their shape and become soggy during cooking.

* Give the courgettes a good wash, cut them into 1cm slices, then halve the slices.

* Proceed with the Basic Risotto recipe and add the courgettes and herbs around 10 minutes into the cooking process.

TOP TIP: You can substitute lots of different veggies for the courgettes. I especially love young broad beans that have been blanched. Add to the risotto, along with a sprig of chopped mint. Peas work well too.

Rice

- Add salt and a little oil to the water to stop the rice from sticking together. Remember to use a large enough saucepan when cooking rice. It grows to three times its original size.

- Allow 75ml uncooked rice per head.

- As a general guide use:
     1 part long grain rice to 2 (and a bit) parts water.
     1 part basmati rice to $1^{1}/_{2}$ to 2 parts water.
     1 part arborio rice to 2 parts stock.

- Measure the rice by volume not weight. For example, pour 150ml long grain rice into a measuring jug. You will then need 300 to 350ml water or stock in which to cook it.

- If the rice is tender and there is still too much liquid, drain it off in a sieve and return the rice to the pan and cover with a piece of kitchen roll. Stand for 3 minutes then fluff with a fork and serve.

- If your rice is still not cooked but looking a little dry, just add more water or stock to the saucepan.

- To enhance the flavour of rice, cook it in a little stock instead of water.

- Don't stir rice while it's simmering, except briefly to ensure it is not sticking to the pan. Basmati and long grain rice have a tendency to break up and go mushy if fiddled with too much.

- When the rice has finished cooking remove the pan from the heat and uncover. Place a sheet of kitchen roll over the top of the saucepan and let the rice 'stand' for 3 or 4 minutes. This enables the rice to plump up and absorb any remaining moisture. Fluff it up with a fork before eating.

- Reheat rice in the microwave.

Italian Rice and Beans

Serves 4
⌘ V SC £1

1 x 425 tin cannellini beans
100ml long grain rice
1 medium onion, chopped
2 cloves garlic, chopped
2 tbs olive oil
1 x 400g tin chopped plum tomatoes
200ml veg stock
Handful of black olives
Pinch of dried chilli
Pinch of dried thyme
Cheddar cheese, grated

- Using a medium/large saucepan, gently sweat the onion and garlic in the olive oil for 5 or 6 minutes.

- Stir in the rice, dried chilli and thyme, tomatoes, stock, and black olives.

- Cover and simmer on medium heat for 10 minutes, stirring from time to time.

- Remove the lid, add the drained beans and continue cooking for another 5 minutes or until the rice is tender and the liquid has been absorbed. Let the rice rest for 3 minutes before eating. Serve with some grated cheddar cheese.

Mince Rice

Serves 4

⌘ **£1**

1 tbs olive oil
1 medium onion, chopped
1 clove garlic, chopped
2 slices bacon, chopped
250g minced beef
200ml arborio rice
1 x 400g tin chopped plum tomatoes
400ml chicken stock
1 tbs ketchup
Pinch of dried thyme

- Sweat the onion and garlic in the olive oil in a large saucepan.

- After 4 or 5 minutes, add the mince and bacon and cook until the meat is browned through.

- Season with salt, pepper and dried thyme.

- Add the tinned tomatoes, stock, ketchup and rice. Give them all a good stir.

- Cover the pan with a lid or foil and simmer for 20 minutes, stirring occasionally.

- Serve with a lump of grated parmesan or cheddar and a green salad.

  TOP TIP: This is delicious warmed up. Warm through in the microwave. Keep as a leftover for up to 3 days but cover well with cling film.

Dirty Rice

Serves 4

⌘ £2

150g smoked bacon, chopped or pancetta cubes
150g chorizo sausage, chopped
1 medium onion, chopped
2 cloves garlic, chopped
1 small green pepper, chopped
1 small red pepper, chopped
1 tsp cayenne pepper
1 tsp ground cumin
200g long grain rice
500ml chicken stock

- Sauté the sausage and bacon pieces in a large saucepan over medium/high heat. Add a splash of oil if necessary.

- Remove the meat to a plate when cooked through and the bacon is slightly crisp.

- Add a splash of olive oil to the same pan and sweat the onion, garlic and peppers for 5 minutes over medium/low heat. Add the cayenne and cumin, and cook, stirring for another few minutes. The kitchen will smell wonderful by now.

- Stir in the rice, cook for a minute then put the pig bits back into the pan along with the stock. Cover and simmer for 12 minutes.

- Add more stock if the dish is becoming too dry.

- When the rice is tender, remove from the heat and let stand, covered, for 3 minutes.

  Top Tip: If you really want to eat up your greens, throw in some frozen peas during the last 2 minutes of cooking.

Stuffed Peppers

Serves 4
£2

1 tbs olive oil
1 medium onion, finely chopped
2 cloves garlic, finely chopped
300g minced lamb or beef
1 mug of pre-cooked rice ($^1/_2$ mug, 100ml, uncooked rice)
50ml red wine or stock
1 x 400g tin chopped tomatoes
4 green or red peppers
1 tsp ground cumin

• Pre-heat oven to 190°C/gas mark 5.

• In a medium saucepan sweat the onion and garlic in olive oil for 4 minutes until translucent. Add the mince and cook until browned.

• Add the red wine, tomatoes, cumin and cooked rice. Give it all a good stir, test for seasoning, then simmer for 8 minutes.

• With the peppers create little vessels into which you can stuff the meat. Cut the tops off and scrape all the seeds out.

• Once the flavour of the rice/meat mixture is to your liking, get stuffing. Spoon $^1/_4$ of the meat mixture into each pepper and put its 'lid' back on.

• Place the peppers in a casserole or ovenproof pan just large enough to hold them snugly. Expertly open the tin of tomatoes and pour, with their juice, all around the peppers. Season and cover the dish with foil.

• Cook in the oven for about 1$^1/_2$ hours or until the peppers are tender.

TOP TIPS: These improve with age so are ideal for making in advance, eating as leftovers or for freezing.

You can convert this into a vegetarian recipe by swapping the mince for a pulse, such as a 400g tin of drained chickpeas or lentils, jazzed up with a teaspoon of crushed coriander seeds.

Pulses

Pulses are unbelievably good value, especially in their dried form, but they need soaking and lengthy simmering so consider the gas/electricity bill and your available time. Being busy folk, you may well opt for tinned every time. However, if you are feeling worthy, very poor or simply want to spend a day chilling at home I will talk you through the dried bean process.

Top Tips:

*   Most beans require around 6 to 8 hours soaking, but there is a short cut: place the beans in a large saucepan and cover with water. Bring the water to the boil, remove from heat and let the beans soak for 2 hours. Drain, add fresh water and simmer until tender.

*   Use a large saucepan when cooking pulses as they greatly increase in volume. Most pulses take around 2 hours to cook.

*   Lentils, bless them, do not require soaking and can be simmered straight from the store cupboard. They generally need less cooking than other pulses, say around 40 minutes, and can be cooked in stock. Like rice, pulses can be measured by volume rather than weight.

*   Puy are the queen of lentils. They are compact in size and have a grey/blue marbled appearance. Puy lentils taste delicious and bear up under almost any culinary abuse.

*   If you are using tinned pulses, beware: they tend to be very well cooked and can turn mushy quite easily. However, this makes them excellent for purées.

*   Pulses are full of protein as well as being an excellent source of carbohydrate. They are the perfect fuel for all night cramming sessions.

*   Pulses can be used to pad out rather meagre amounts of meat or fish.

*   Dried pulses can be stored in their original packaging or in an airtight container for months on end.

*   Apart from lentils, never add salt or powdered stock to pulses while simmering as this will make them tough. Only season with salt and pepper once cooked. Add a spoonful of bicarbonate of soda during cooking to soften the skins.

Lentils Puy Style

Serves 4
⌘ **£1**

1 tbs olive oil
1 onion, finely chopped
¹/₂ carrot, finely diced
1 clove garlic, finely minced
60g bacon or pancetta, cubed
250ml Puy lentils
750ml stock

- Place the bacon in a medium/large saucepan with the olive oil. Sauté for 2 minutes then add the onion, carrot and garlic.

- Sweat the vegetables for 5 minutes then add the lentils and the stock and bring to a simmer.

- Cook uncovered for approximately 35 minutes, adding more water if necessary.

- The lentils should be tender yet still holding their shape.

Basic Brown Lentils

Serves 4

⌘ V £1

250ml brown lentils
1 onion cut in quarters
1 clove garlic
Pinch of dried thyme
1 1/2 litres water or stock

- Place all the ingredients in a medium/large saucepan and bring to a simmer.

- Cook, uncovered, for 30 minutes then taste to see if the lentils are tender.

- Add more water and cook for longer if necessary.

- When the lentils are tender, drain off any remaining water. Discard the onion and garlic, season and add a splash of olive oil.

Lentils Love:

Olives	Bacon
Onions	Chicken
Tomatoes	Duck
Goats Cheese	Cod
Feta Cheese	Smoked Haddock
Parsley	Mint

Top Tips: Try adding vinaigrette, a few black olives, some crumbled goats cheese and chopped fresh mint to your lentils. Or dress brown lentils with vinaigrette, sliced tomatoes and red onion.

Lentils Puy Style with Chicken Breasts

Serves 4
⌘ **£3**

4 chicken breasts
2 tbs Dijon mustard
2 tbs olive oil
Juice of 1 lemon
2 cloves garlic, sliced
Cooked lentils Puy style (see recipe on p.48)
Pinch of dried chilli
Pinch of dried rosemary

- Begin by marinating the chicken breasts. To do this, place all the ingredients (except the lentils of course) in a plastic bag, secure the top and give the whole lot a good mix around. Leave the chicken to marinate in the bag for at least 1 hour but the longer the better.

- When you are ready to eat, remove the chicken from its marinade and give it a dusting of salt and pepper.

- Heat a frying pan and throw in the chicken breasts. Cook over medium/low heat for 6 minutes per side or until the chicken is no longer pink but still springy to the touch.

- Heat the lentils and serve on a large, warm plate. Top with the chicken.

- Have wedges of lemon and a bottle of olive oil on hand.

  Top Tips: If your breasts are very large you may only need three. Simply cut the cooked chicken into slices and arrange on the lentils.

  Marinated chicken breasts are also good served at room temperature sliced over a Caesar salad.

Sausages with Lentils

Serves 4
£2

8 sausages
Cooked lentils Puy style (see recipe on p.48)
1 x 400g tin chopped plum tomatoes

- Pre-heat oven to 200°C/gas mark 6.

- Place the sausages in a frying pan with a dash of oil. Brown them over a fairly aggressive heat. A lid could be an option for this exercise.

- Add the tomatoes to the cooked lentils. Mix together and warm through. Place the tomatoey lentils in a baking dish.

- When the sausages are looking nicely bronzed, nestle them in amongst the lentils.

- Put the baking dish in the oven and cook for 20 to 30 minutes.

- If the lentils are looking a tad on the dry side, add a dribble of stock.

Eggs

In terms of culinary survival, eggs are a major way forward. They're versatile, full of protein, relatively cheap and can be stored in the fridge for up to two weeks.

Buying

These days most shops offer the choice of both barn eggs and free-range. Some shops are now stocking organic eggs as well. Basically, free-range hens can cluck about in open-air runs while their less lucky sisters are made to perch in an enclosed barn. Organic eggs come from hens raised in open-air runs in areas free from pesticides. The hens also eat a diet of pesticide-free food. In general, the freer the bird the more expensive the egg. The choice is yours.

Storing

Although it is better to cook with eggs at room temperature, it is safer to store them in a cool place such as the refrigerator. Keep the eggs in their box as they can actually pick up nasty smells (which of course your fridge will be free of…) through their shells. If you can be bothered to think about it (I can't), place the eggs in their box pointed end down; this helps them remain fresh longer.

Freshness

Eggs bought from shops have a sell-by date stamped on the box, sometimes right on the egg itself. If you can buy fresh farm eggs with no sell-by date there is a foolproof test you can do for freshness:

- Fill a jug with cold water and gently lower your egg into it. If the egg remains horizontal it's fresh, no worries. If the egg tilts slightly towards the vertical, it is not in its first flush of youth, but it will not kill you.

- If the egg floats into a fully vertical position it is definitely no spring chicken, and must be tossed immediately.

Boiling an egg

I know Delia has already done it, but boiling an egg really does take a certain degree of expertise. So here it is: the art of egg boiling.

- Try to bring your eggs to room temperature. The shock of placing a cold egg into boiling water can cause serious crackage.

- Use a saucepan that holds the eggs snugly. You don't want the eggs to rattle around madly in the boiling water and break. Consider giving your egg a small prick in its broad side. This allows trapped air to escape and prevents cracking.

- Bring the water to a fairly assertive simmer and gently lower the eggs into the saucepan.

Be sure you use enough water to thoroughly cover the eggs.

Timing

Soft boiled	4 minutes
Medium	6 to 7 minutes
Hard boiled	10 to 12 minutes

Be careful not to over-boil an egg. The white will be rubbery and the outer yolk blackish.

Peeling

Place the saucepan containing your eggs in the sink and let cold water wash over them. This will stop the cooking, make peeling easier and save your fingers from certain pain and misery.

Next, remove one egg at a time and gently crack it all over. With the cold tap still running, begin removing the shell, washing away any unwelcome bits. The fresher the egg the harder it will be to peel, but persevere, it will be worth the effort.

Hard boiled and Mollet eggs can be stored for 4 days in the fridge.

Baked Eggs

Serves 2
V £1

4 eggs
30g butter
75g or ¹/₂ cup Cheddar cheese, grated
Bread for toasting
50ml cream or milk

- Pre-heat oven to 190°C /gas mark 5.

- Break the eggs into four ramekins or any other similarly shaped ovenproof container. On top of each egg add some cream or milk and a sprinkling of cheese. Divide the butter into four equal knobs and place one on each egg, then season.

- Place ramekins in a roasting pan and pour boiling water into the pan until half way up the ramekin sides.

- Put pan in the oven and cook for 8 to 12 minutes. The cooking time varies according to the size of container you choose and the amount of garnish used.

- Remove from the oven and let stand in the water for a further 2 minutes while you wait for your bread to toast.

- Place the ramekins on a plate with pieces of buttered toast.

  TOP TIPS: Gammon pieces, salsa, cheese, Worcestershire sauce, cooked pepper, crumbled bacon, and sautéed mushrooms are great garnishes. Place any of them in the bottom of the ramekin before adding the egg.

  Eggs work a charm cooked in the microwave. Prepare your eggs as above then microwave on full power for 30 seconds per egg, 40 seconds for two. I would advise you to microwave only two at a time.

  Beware when microwaving: give the yolk a gentle prick with a sharp object or an explosion is certain to occur, and I don't mean maybe.

Frittatas

A frittata is basically an open-faced Italian style omelette. The ingredients are the same as in an ordinary omelette but the technique is far simpler. The eggs are added to the filling in a frying pan and cooked extremely slowly with no folding required. The perfect frittata should have a firm underside with a moist top and centre.

The beauty of a frittata is that it can be eaten piping hot straight from the frying pan or at room temperature at some later date.

TOP TIPS:

- If you want to make a frittata for only two, halve the ingredients, obviously, and try to use a smaller frying pan. The cooking time will also be slightly less.

- You can more or less fill a frittata with anything. Simply follow the directions given in the Ham and Cheese Frittata recipe opposite replacing the pig bits with any of the following:

Sautéed mushrooms
Onions
Spinach
Courgettes
Peppers
Tomatoes
Salsa
Leftover potatoes
Sun dried tomatoes

Ham and Cheese Frittata

Serves 4
⌘ £1

8 eggs
150 to 200g gammon, bacon or pancetta, cubed or chopped
2 tbs olive oil
25g butter
125g Cheddar cheese, grated

- Begin by placing the oil, butter and pig of choice in a 22 to 25cm frying pan. Place over medium heat and sauté until the bacon/ham is cooked through.

- Place the eggs in a small mixing bowl and give them a good whisk. Season.

- Pour the eggs over the bacon/ham and scatter the cheese evenly over the top.

- Cook over the lowest heat possible for 10 to 12 minutes.

- Turn your grill to its highest setting and cook the fritatta for 1 minute to firm up any liquid egg. Don't panic if you are grill-less, the Frittata will still be yummy, just a tad looser on top.

- Cut into wedges and serve warm.

Spinach Frittata

Serves 4
⌘ V £1

200g fresh or frozen spinach
Pinch of grated nutmeg
8 large eggs
1 onion, finely chopped
1 clove garlic, finely chopped
2 tbs olive oil
25g butter
125g Cheddar cheese, grated

- If you are using fresh spinach, cook for 2 minutes in rapidly boiling water, drain, chop and squeeze dry. If you are using frozen spinach, defrost, drain and give this variety a good squeeze as well. Spinach retains an enormous amount of water, so keep this in mind.

- Place the onion and garlic in a 25cm frying pan along with the oil and butter. Gently sweat for 5 minutes and add the drained spinach. Season and sprinkle over the nutmeg.

- Mix the eggs in a small bowl and season.

- Pour the eggs over the spinach in the frying pan, scatter on the cheese and cook over the lowest heat possible for around 10 to 12 minutes.

- Place the frittata under a fierce grill and cook for a further minute just to firm up any loose egg on the top.

Corned Beef Hash

Serves 4
⌘ £1

4 eggs
1 x 325g tin corned beef
2 potatoes
1 onion, finely chopped
2 tbs olive oil
1 tsp Worcestershire sauce
1 tsp Grain mustard

- Extract the beef from its tin and chop into 3cm pieces.

- Peel the potatoes, cut into similar sized chunks and simmer in boiling water until tender.

- Cook the onion in the olive oil for 5 minutes before adding the potatoes and corned beef. Fry over medium/high heat, letting the potatoes become hash-brownish.

- Add the mustard and Worcestershire sauce to the hash, then season to taste. Divide into four bowls.

- Fry the eggs in a slosh of oil and a knob of butter then serve the corned beef hash topped with one egg per serving and a bottle of ketchup poised for action.

French Toast (Eggy Bread)

Serves 4
⌘ V £1

6 to 8 thick slices of white bread
4 eggs
150ml full cream milk
40g butter

- Pre-heat oven to 140°C/gas mark 1.

- Place half the butter in a large frying pan over medium heat.

- Whisk the eggs and milk together in a dish large enough to hold a slice of bread. Dip the bread into the egg mixture one piece at a time, ensuring the bread is thoroughly coated.

- When the butter is sizzling, but not brown, add the eggy bread. Wedge in a couple of pieces if you can and cook for around 3 minutes per side. You should be aiming at French toast that is nicely browned on the outside and soft inside.

- Put the toast on a plate and keep warm in the oven while you cook the remaining pieces.

- Add more butter to the pan before making your next lot of French toast.

- Serve up on warm plates with loads of butter and one of the following: maple syrup, blueberries, jam, cinnamon sugar, banana, raisins, bacon, strawberries or icing sugar.

    TOP TIP: Use pannetonne or raisin bread as a treat.

American-style Pancakes

Serves 4
⌘ V £1

200g plain flour
2$^1/_2$ tsp baking powder
2 eggs
275ml milk
50g melted butter
2 tbs vegetable oil
1 tsp sugar

- Pre-heat oven to 140°C/gas mark 1.

- Sift all the dry ingredients into a mixing bowl. Add the eggs, sugar and butter then slowly pour in the milk a little at a time, stirring with a wooden spoon. Begin with a thick paste then gradually thin it out with the remaining milk to achieve a smooth batter. Do not worry about the odd lump. Do not whisk the mixture or it will become glutinous and tough.

- Place a large frying pan over medium/high heat and, using a piece of kitchen roll, wipe its bottom with a thin veil of vegetable oil.

- When the oil looks hot and hazy pour $^1/_2$ ladleful of batter into the pan. Fit in as many pancakes as you can, at least 2 at a time.

- When little bubbles begin to appear, after 1 or 2 minutes, turn the pancake over using a spatula.

- Cook on the other side for a minute, or until golden brown.

- Keep the pancakes in the preheated oven while you make a batch. You may need to give the pan another wiping of oil between batches.

   TOP TIPS: Batter can be stored, covered, in the fridge for up to two days.

   Pancakes are great with maple syrup, eggs, bacon, berries, butter, banana or coconut.

Able Veg

Salads

Top Tips:

- Buy salad leaves from the greengrocer or street market on an as-you-need-it basis. Avoid the pre-packed varieties as they are super-expensive, as well as being less fresh. Store any unused salad leaves in a plastic shopping bag, tied at the top, in the fridge.

- Always wash your lettuce. Rinse each leaf under cold running water and dry by bundling it into a tea towel, gathering it into a parcel then spinning it around over your head. I strongly recommend you do this outside, or out of a window.

- Make a large jar of vinaigrette (see p.64) and store in the refrigerator. Always wait until you are ready to sit down before dressing your salad with vinaigrette. The lettuce will wilt if dressed too early.

- Make salad more exciting by usign different types of leaves. Consider:
  round lettuce
  frisee lettuce
  cos lettuce
  oak leaf lettuce
  escarole
  rocket
  chicory
  watercress

- And as well as the usual tomato and cucumber, try adding:
  pumpkin seeds
  walnuts
  sunflower seeds
  parmesan cheese
  blue cheese
  feta cheese
  sprouts
  red onion
  bacon bits

All seeds and nuts taste better if salted and lightly toasted in the oven at 180°C/gas mark 4, for 4 to 5 minutes. Be careful not to burn them!

Basic Vinaigrette

180ml olive oil
50ml red wine vinegar
2 tsp Dijon or English mustard
1 tsp salt & pepper

Parmesan Vinaigrette

180ml olive oil
50ml red wine vinegar
1 tsp Dijon mustard
2 tbs grated Parmesan

Garlic Vinaigrette

180ml olive oil
50ml red wine vinegar
1 tsp Dijon mustard
1 clove garlic, peeled and halved

Honey Mustard Vinaigrette

180ml olive oil
50 ml red wine vinegar
1 tsp grain mustard
1 tsp honey

The technique is the same for all these recipes.

- Place all the ingredients in an empty jam jar and give the whole lot a good shaking.

- Alternatively, place the mustard, seasoning and vinegar in a bowl and whisk together using a fork. Still whisking, slowly pour in the olive oil.

Greek Salad

Serves 4
V £2

1 Iceberg or Cos lettuce
1 x 200g Feta cheese
Handful of Kalamata olives
$1/2$ cucumber, thinly sliced
2 sprigs of mint, chopped
2 tomatoes, sliced, or 12 cherry tomatoes
$1/2$ recipe of Garlic Vinaigrette (see opposite)

- Wash the lettuce and place in a large salad bowl.

- Top with the remaining ingredients and give a good toss. Dress with the garlic vinaigrette.

Spinach Salad

Serves 4
£2

250g fresh spinach
Handful of walnuts, toasted
150g Danish blue cheese, crumbled
4 slices smoked bacon
2 eggs
$1/2$ recipe of Basic Vinaigrette (see opposite)

- Boil the eggs for 10 minutes. Peel and cut them into quarters. Set to one side.

- Meanwhile grill the bacon until crisp, then crumble into small pieces.

- Wash the spinach and place in a salad bowl. Add the eggs, bacon and remaining ingredients. Dress with the basic vinaigrette and gently toss, preferably using your hands.

Caesar Salad

Serves 4
⌘ V £2

1 clove garlic, sliced
1 tbs salt
Juice of 1/2 lemon
1 tbs vinegar
2 tsps English mustard
1 x 50g tin anchovies
120ml olive oil
Shake of Tabasco
1 large Cos lettuce
1 egg
50g Parmesan, grated

- Clean the lettuce in cold water and dry in a spinner or tea towel.

- Boil the egg for 1 minute only, and remove from water.

- Cut the garlic into thin slices on a chopping board. Sprinkle with 1 tbs salt then mash it into a pulp with the back of a fork.

- Place the mashed garlic in a salad bowl and add the mustard, lemon juice, vinegar, Tabasco and mix together.

- Pour the olive oil into the salad bowl in a slow stream, whisking as you pour.

- Make a small hole in the top of the egg and scoop the 'flesh' out into the dressing mixture.

- Give the dressing a good stir, then throw in the lettuce and toss until it's well coated. Drain the oil off the anchovies, chop them into quarters and scatter all over the salad.

- Grate some Parmesan over the top of the salad and get stuck in.

  Top Tip: Iceberg lettuce makes this dish much more wallet friendly.

Warm Salad of Chicken Livers and Bacon

Serves 4
⌘ £2

Lettuce of choice
250g chicken livers
8 rashers smoked bacon
250g French beans
1 tbs butter
Slosh of olive oil
$^1/_2$ vinaigrette recipe (see p.64)

- Grill or fry the bacon until crisp then break up into pieces on a plate.

- Top and tail the beans and throw them into boiling salted water. Cover and cook for 3 minutes, making certain they stay crisp. Drain the beans and give them a refreshing shower of cold water. Place to one side and pat them dry with a sheet of kitchen roll.

- Wash the lettuce in cold water and dry in a spinner or a tea towel.

- Place the olive oil and butter in a frying pan. Cut the livers into 1cm strips removing any gristly membraney bits. Season.

- Sauté the livers over medium heat for 2 or 3 minutes. The insides should still be slightly pink.

- Place the lettuce on 4 plates.

- Divide the liver, bacon and beans between the 4 plates as evenly as possible, but naturally allowing more bacon for the cook.

- Dress the salads with vinaigrette.

   Top Tip: I like to use a round lettuce mixed with a head of radicchio. This gives the salad a bit of festive colour.

Couscous

Serves 4
⌘ V £1

300ml couscous
450ml hot vegetable stock

• Place the couscous in a medium sized bowl. Pour the stock over it and cover with kitchen roll or tea towel. Leave for 5 minutes and fluff with a fork.

• Serve warm as is, or as a salad with a little vinaigrette and one or more of the following: chopped cucumber, chopped tomato, cumin, roast peppers, coriander seeds, red onion slices, parsley, chopped peppers, basil, chopped fennel, chilli, mint, feta cheese, goats cheese, diced courgettes.

Richard's Favourite Dressing

Serves 4

100ml olive oil
2 tbs tomato purée
Juice of 1/2 lemon
1 tbs cumin
1/2 tsp cayenne pepper

• Place all the ingredients in a jar and give it a vigorous shake.

• This dressing is especially good served on couscous topped with roast veggies and feta or goats cheese. At its best along side a roast chicken.

TOP TIPS:
We live off couscous in our household. It is so simple to make it is almost a joke. Couscous is also low fat, an excellent salad base, vegetarian and boringly goody-goody in almost every way.

Roast Potatoes

Serves 4 to 5
V £1

1 kilo Desiree or Maris Piper potatoes
$1/2$ cup olive oil
2 tbs salt

- Pre-heat oven to 200°C/gas mark 6.

- Peel the potatoes and cut into even sized pieces, say 4 to 5cm.

- Place in a large pot of boiling water and simmer for 6 minutes, or until the edges of the potatoes are becoming fluffy.

- Tip the water out of the pan using the lid to keep the potatoes from falling out.

- Wedge the lid firmly on the pot and give the potatoes hell by shaking them like fury. This is not just therapy. It makes the potatoes fluffy on the outside so they become lovely and crispy during cooking.

- Pour enough oil into a roasting tin to cover its bottom by $1/2$cm. Place tin in oven to heat for 5 minutes.

- Remove the roasting tin from the oven and add the shaken and confused potatoes.

- Give the potatoes a liberal sprinkling of salt and cook for 1 hour or until they are beautifully bronzed. Consider turning them during cooking to ensure an all over tan.

- Eat the potatoes as soon as they are ready. They will lose their crispiness if left waiting.

    TOP TIP: Leftover roast potatoes can be kept and used in frittatas and fry-ups. Sautéed potatoes, gammon and eggs make a great Sunday supper.

Cheesy Baked Potatoes

Serves 4 to 6
V £1

1 kilo King Edward potatoes
350ml milk
1 clove garlic, peeled
125g Cheddar cheese, grated
75g butter

- Pre-heat oven to 190°C/gas mark 5.

- Place the milk in a small saucepan. Peel the garlic, cut it in half and submerge it in the milk.

- Gently heat the milk then set to one side. This allows the garlic to flavour (infuse) the milk.

- Peel the potatoes then slice as thinly as possible.

- Once you have peeled the potatoes use them straight away so they don't brown.

- Butter the bottom of a baking dish (measuring 25cm x 20cm-ish). Place a layer of potatoes on the bottom of the dish and season.

- Continue building up the potatoes, seasoning and adding 'nuts' of butter as you go, layer by layer.

- When you have used up all the potatoes pour the milk into the baking dish, binning the garlic.

- Season the final layer, add a few more 'nuts' of butter, then grate the cheese over the top.

- Bake the potatoes for 50 to 60 minutes. You may want to place a roasting tin under the potatoes to catch any overflow. After an hour the top should be brown with melted cheese and the centre soft when pierced with a knife. If the top is becoming too brown place a piece of foil loosely over the top of the dish.

TOP TIPS: You can peel the potatoes ahead of time then place them in a bowl of cold water to stop them from going brown. Pad this dish out into a meal by adding a few thin slices of gammon or smoked haddock between the layers of potato.

Potato Skins

Serves 4
V SC £1

3 or 4 potatoes, Maris Piper, Desiree or King Edward
4 tbs sea salt
4 tbs olive oil

- Pre-heat oven to 220°C/gas mark 7.

- Wash the potatoes and dry thoroughly. Cut them into quarters and place on a roasting tin. Dry them again.

- Rub the potato chunks with olive oil and loads of salt.

- Cook for 30 to 40 minutes, turning the potatoes occasionally to crisp them up all over.

   Top Tips: Top with any or all the following:

   Cheddar cheese, grated
   Bacon bits
   Black olives
   Salsa
   Soured cream
   Jalapeno peppers
   Sautéed mushrooms

   My gang adore potato skins, which is just fine by me. They have the triple advantage of being easy, inexpensive and the healthiest part of the potato.

Marvellous Mash

Serves 4 to 6
V £1

1 kilo King Edward potatoes
7 to 8 tbs milk
60g butter

- Put a large pot of water on to boil.

- Peel the potatoes and cut into even sized chunks of 5cm or so.

- Put the potatoes in to simmer for 15 to 20 minutes. Do not boil or they will turn to mush.

- Poke the fattest potato to see if it is cooked. If it offers any resistance, cook for another 5 minutes.

- Drain the potatoes and put a lid or tea towel over the top. Leave the potatoes to rest for 5 minutes. This makes them more mashable.

- Give the potatoes a good pounding with a masher to break up any lumpy bits.

- Add the butter and continue mashing away until it has melted.

- Finally add the milk and give the whole lot hell. I am serious; you must treat this recipe as an upper arm exercise in disguise. Really go to town beating the potatoes into a smooth, lump free mound. Add salt to taste.

Top Tip: Mash is great with one of the following toppings: 2 tbs grain mustard; 250g grated Cheddar cheese; 2 tbs horseradish; 3 finely sliced spring onions; 120g pesto.

Wensleydale Garlic Mushrooms

Serves 4
V £1

400g button mushrooms
1 tbs olive oil
80g butter
2 cloves garlic, finely chopped
200g Wensleydale cheese

- Clean the mushrooms. Because mushrooms are grown in sterile compost you needn't worry too much about the odd speck of dirt.

- Never wash mushrooms, they will become totally water logged and nasty. Simply peel off the outer layer of their caps or gently dust them with a piece of kitchen roll. Most mushrooms come looking depressingly clean these days anyway. Cut in half if they are a bit large.

- Put the olive oil and half the butter in a frying pan and place on a fairly high heat. Be careful not to brown the butter.

- When the butter has melted and is sizzling, throw in the mushrooms and sauté, stirring constantly for 3 minutes. You may want to cook them in two batches, depending on the size of your pan. Season.

- Turn the grill on to its highest setting.

- Turn down the heat on the burner and add the garlic, remaining butter and the first load of mushrooms (if cooked in batches). Cook for another minute, stirring all the while. Remove from burner.

- Grate the cheese over the mushrooms and pop the pan under the grill.

- Grill the dish until the cheese is bubbling and brown.

- Serve the mushrooms straight from the frying pan with loads of bread to absorb the garlicky butter.

Roast Red Peppers

Serves 4
V £1

4 red peppers, halved
4 tbs olive oil
2 cloves garlic, sliced
2 ripe tomatoes, cut in halves

- Pre-heat oven to 200°C/gas mark 6.

- Cut the peppers in half, lengthways, and remove the white pith and seeds.

- Peel the garlic and cut into thin slivers.

- Place the peppers in a roasting tin, cut side facing up. Divide the garlic evenly between the peppers.

- Adorn each pepper with a tomato 'cap' and pour the oil all over.

- Season and roast in the oven for 50 to 60 minutes.

- For variety, choose any of the following to perk up your peppers: shredded basil, one leaf per pepper; anchovy fillets, one fillet per pepper; sun-dried tomatoes, one per pepper. Simply slip them between the pepper and its tomato topping before you bung them in the oven.

  Top Tips: Serve peppers with a green salad and masses of crusty bread, like Italian ciabatta.

  Roast peppers are delicious at room temperature and make great leftovers.

Roast Summer and Winter Veg

Serves 4
Winter
V £1

2 red onions
3 carrots
2 parsnips, peeled
1 swede
2 potatoes, peeled
3 cloves garlic, unpeeled and halved
$1/2$ cup olive oil

Serves 4
Summer
V £2

2 red peppers, deseeded
2 red onions
1 fennel, core removed
3 medium-sized courgettes
1 firm aubergine
2 cloves garlic, peeled and halved
$1/2$ cup olive oil

- Pre-heat oven to 200°C/gas mark 6.

- Cut all the ingredients into evenish sized hunks.

- Chuck everything in a roasting tin and pour on the oil.

- Toss together to ensure everything gets its fair share of the oil. Season well.

- Cook for around 45 to 60 minutes, turning occasionally.

TOP TIPS: Summer roast vegetables are delicious on couscous, pasta or a toasted baguette. Go ahead and use up whatever veggies come to hand. Roast veg is excellent to cook along with roast chicken or roast pork.

Fish Dish

Fish is so good for you I would love to think you were eating it at least twice a week.

Loads of clever folk tell me they are frightened of cooking fish. There is no need to be. Just hold my hand and I'll take you over the hurdles.

TOP TIPS:

- Try to buy all your fish 'wet'. This means fresh from a fishmonger or the fresh fish department of a supermarket. Always ask the fishmonger to do any necessary preparation; if he refuses, find another one. Avoid pre-packed fish if at all possible.

- Really fresh fish should have shiny, full eyes. If the eyes look dull and sunken it is probably getting on a bit. Ask your fishmonger how long it is safe to store the fish before eating. You should really eat fish on day one or day two.

- Fresh fish should not smell 'fishy'.

- Store fish in cling film in the coldest part of your fridge.

- Some fish freezes very well. Generally the firm flesh fish freezes better than flat fish. Smoked haddock, cod and salmon freeze very well.

- To freeze fish, buy while still fresh then wrap it in cling film. Don't forget to label, date and freeze. The fish should be just fine for up to 4 weeks.

- Frozen fish defrosts quite quickly. Place the frozen fish in the fridge to defrost while you are out for the day.

- Try very hard not to overcook fish. It is easy to do as fish often continues cooking even when off the heat. Be on the safe side and undercook. You can always cook the fish a bit longer if necessary.

- Always test fish for doneness by probing it with a fork. Properly cooked fish should flake away with ease but still hold itself together. If the fish is squidgy or refuses to flake I would give it a bit longer in the heat.

Smoked Haddock with Spicy Lentils

Serves 4
⌘ V £3

4 x 150g pieces smoked haddock, skinned & boned
1 clove garlic, finely minced
1 onion, finely chopped
1 tbs olive oil
1 x 400g tin chopped plum tomatoes
250g Puy lentils
1 tbs coriander seeds, crushed
1/2 tbs cardamom pods, crushed
1tsp dried chilli
1 tbs Thai fish sauce
700ml water or veg stock
Bunch of fresh coriander, torn

- Place the oil, onion and garlic in a large saucepan. Cook over medium/low heat for 5 minutes or until translucent but not browned.

- Crush the coriander and cardamom in a plastic bag, hitting with a blunt object such as a tin of baked beans or your head. Throw away the cardamom husks.

- Add the spices, including the chilli, to the onion mixture and cook for another minute or so. The kitchen should smell wonderful.

- Add the tomatoes, lentils, fish sauce and water. Simmer for around 35 minutes. Add more water if necessary. The lentils should hold shape in a moist mass but not be watery.

- Taste, adding seasoning if required. The fish sauce is quite salty so you may not need to add anything more.

- Place the fish in a frying pan and pour over enough milk or water to cover it.

- Bring the milk/water to a gentle simmer, then poach for around 5 minutes.

- The fish should flake without resistance but still hold together. If it's still rubbery and translucent, give it another 2 minutes.

- Serve the fish on a mound of warmed spicy lentils. Give the fish a drizzle of olive oil and the whole dish a good scattering of torn fresh coriander.

Cod with Olives and Sweet Peppers

Serves 4
V £3

4 x 150g pieces cod
2 red peppers, sliced
1 onion, sliced
1 clove garlic, chopped
1 tbs capers
20 (ish) black olives
4 tbs olive oil
1 lemon

- Pre-heat oven to 220°C/gas mark 7.

- Peel the onion and cut in half. With its cut side facing down slice into thin half slices.

- Cut the red peppers in half, remove the seeds and stalk, and cut into long thin slices.

- Put 2 tbs olive oil into a medium saucepan. Add the onion and peppers and cook over medium/high heat for 12 to 15 minutes. The peppers should be soft and slightly browned.

- Add the chopped garlic, olives and capers and cook over low heat for another minute.

- Put the remaining olive oil in a roasting pan and add the cod. Season well.

- Cook the fish for 8 minutes or until it flakes easily and is no longer translucent.

- Serve the fish on warmed plates with the peppers and a wedge of lemon.

  Top Tip: New potatoes or crusty bread go well with this dish.

Salmon with Black Beans

Serves 4
⌘ V £3

2 x 425g tins black beans
4 x 150g salmon fillets, 4cm thick
3 tbs vegetable oil
8 tbs soy sauce
2 tbs fresh ginger, finely chopped
2 cloves garlic, finely chopped
Pinch of dried chilli
1 lime
Bunch of fresh coriander, torn

- Drain the beans and place in a bowl. Put the oil, ginger, garlic, chilli and soy sauce in a jug and mix. Pour half the sauce over the beans.

- Marinate the salmon in a plastic bag containing the remaining sauce. An hour should just about do it.

- Remove the salmon from the marinade and pat dry with a paper towel. Pack a generous amount of salt onto the skin side. This will make it yummy and crunchy.

- Place your frying pan over a fairly high temperature, add an additional tablespoon of vegetable oil and cook the salmon, skin side down, for 4 minutes.

- Turn off the heat, flip the fish over and cook for 2 minutes on the flesh side. The pan will remain hot. Let the fish rest in the pan for a further minute or two.

- The time needed to cook the salmon will vary according to its thickness. The salmon might initially appear underdone but it will continue to cook for a few minutes once out of the frying pan.

- Serve the salmon with wedges of lime, torn coriander, the black beans and some crunchy fresh green broccoli.

  Top Tip: You can serve the salmon with plain basmati rice if the beans are too much of a sweat.

Smoked Haddock with Mustard Mash

Serves 4
V £2

4 x 150g smoked haddock
1 x recipe Marvellous Mash (see p.72)
1 tbs grain mustard
75g butter
100g Gruyère cheese, grated

- Pre-heat oven to 220°C/gas mark 7.

- Make a batch of Marvellous Mash or use some leftovers.

- Add the mustard to the potatoes, mix thoroughly and warm through if necessary.

- Place the pieces of fish in a roasting tin or baking dish and season with freshly ground pepper.

- Top each piece of fish with a dollop of butter then pile on a hearty portion of potato. Divide the cheese evenly between all four.

- Cook for 10 to 12 minutes then place under the grill for 2 minutes to brown up the cheese a bit.

Top Tips: You can use leftover potatoes for this recipe. Simply add the mustard and possibly a tablespoon of milk. Use Cheddar cheese if you can't get your hands on Gruyère.

This is so delicious I beg you to try it. I think of it as a lazy man's Fish Pie.

Cock and Bull Stories

Chicken

Dishes made with chicken should and will become an invaluable part of your cooking repertoire. Chicken is inexpensive, easy to come by, simple to roast, great to pick at and can lend itself to masses of recipes.

TOP TIPS:

- A free range chicken is really much more expensive than her barn reared cousin. Unless you are feeling very flush I would recommend you enjoy the (admittedly tastier) free range on special occasions only, and buy barn reared for everyday.

- Always take the chicken out of her plastic wrapping and store her in greaseproof paper instead. The plastic can cause the chicken to sweat and go off. Note her sell-by date on the paper or in your head.

- Before cooking your chicken give her a good rinse, inside and out, under the cold tap. Pat her dry with a few pieces of kitchen roll.

- If you are saving cooked chicken for leftovers make sure she has totally cooled off before you put her in the fridge. Be certain to cover any cooled leftover chicken with cling film (okay once cooked) or foil.

- Cooked chicken should be safe to eat for up to 3 days if properly stored in the fridge.

- Think about roasting a chicken every week to generally pick at, use in other recipes and make sandwiches with.

- Avoid buying a pre-frozen chicken. It is better to buy a fresh chicken and freeze resplendent in her wrapping. She will be quite happy for 4 months in the deep freeze.

- To defrost a chicken, take off her wrapping and leave her in the kitchen while you are out for the day.

Chicken with Lemon and Olives

Serves 4
⌘ **£2**

8 chicken thighs
2 tbs vegetable oil
400ml stock
Handful of black olives
Handful of green olives
2 yellow peppers, sliced
2 lemons, sliced
1 tsp ground cumin

- Pour the oil into a frying pan and set over medium heat.

- Add the chicken and season.

- Brown the chicken on both sides. Use a lid during this process because the chicken is certain to spit at you.

- Add the pepper slices and cumin then continue sautéing for 2 minutes or until the peppers become slightly browned as well.

- Add the olives and lemons and pour in the stock.

- Simmer uncovered for 20 minutes.

- Serve with couscous or rice.

Sin Chicken

Serves 4
⌘ £2

3 chicken breasts, in 2cm slices
2 tbs vegetable oil
2 cloves garlic, crushed
1 tbs chopped ginger
150ml stock
5 tbs hoi sin sauce
1 tbs soy sauce
1 red pepper, sliced

- Pour the oil into a frying pan and place over a medium heat.

- Stir-fry the chicken and pepper for 2 minutes.

- Add the garlic and ginger and cook for another minute.

- Add the stock and sauces. Simmer uncovered for 4 minutes.

- Remove the chicken and peppers to a plate with a slotted spoon.

- Let the sauce continue simmering for another minute or two, until it thickens.

- Return the chicken to the pan and warm through in the sauce.

- Serve with plain boiled rice and crunchy, barely cooked, broccoli.

Fast Roast Chicken

Serves 4
£2

1 x 1 1/2 kilo chicken
75g butter, room temperature
1 lemon
1 clove garlic
Herbs of choice

- Pre-heat oven to 220°C/gas mark 7.

- Unbind the chicken's legs and give her a good wash out under the tap. Dry her off with a few pieces of kitchen roll.

- Place the chicken right side up in a roasting tin and smear the butter all over, particularly the breasts.

- Cut the lemon in half and squeeze the juice all over the chicken. Stuff the squeezed out lemon halves up her bottom, along with the herbs and the clove of garlic.

- Season the chicken generously.

- Cook for 1 hour. Prick the thigh to test for doneness. If the juices still run pink cook for another 10 minutes and test again.

- Open the oven door and let the chicken rest for 10 to 15 minutes before carving. This helps the meat to relax.

- Tip the chicken so she looks as though she's standing upright and let the juices flow from her cavity.

- Remove the chicken to a warm plate. Place the roasting tin over a low heat and scrape the crunchy bits off the bottom.

- Pour the warm juices from the tin into a jug and serve with the chicken. This recipe doesn't need gravy as the buttery juices speak for themselves. To prevent the juices from separating give them a serious whisking.

- For a simple Sunday lunch that's hard to beat, serve with a green salad and an enormous amount of couscous.

Top Tips: This recipe is very good served at room temperature or eaten cold in sandwiches. It is also delicious when combined with the following recipes:

Pesto Risotto (p.37)
Italian Rice and Beans (p.43)
Lentil Puy Style (p.48)
Brown lentils (p.49)
Couscous Salad (p.68)

Caesar Salad (p.66)
Spinach Salad (p.65)
Roast Red Peppers (p.74)
Roast Summer and
Winter Veg (p. 75)

If you want to roast a chicken along with a dish that requires a lower temperature that's fine. Simply allow the chicken a little extra cooking time.

Traditional Roast Chicken

Serves 4
£2

1 x 1 1/2 kilo chicken
40g butter
8 rashers of streaky bacon
1 onion, peeled
1 lemon
8 chipolatas
1 tbs flour
400 ml stock

- Pre-heat oven to 190°C/gas mark 5.

- Untie the chicken and give her a good rinse under the cold tap. Pat her dry with a few pieces of kitchen roll.

- Place the chicken in a roasting tin right way up. Smear the butter all over, concentrating on the breasts. Season well.

- Prick the lemon all over with a fork and stuff it up her bottom, along with the onion. If they won't both fit, use half of each.

- Carefully arrange the bacon in an overlapping fashion so the chicken appears to be wearing a stripy leotard.

- Cook for 20 minutes per 450g, plus 15 minutes extra. So your 1 1/2 kilo bird should be cooked in 1 hour 15 minutes.

- After 45 minutes remove the bacon from the chicken so she can brown up a tad. Keep the bacon somewhere warm.

- While you are removing the bacon add the chipolatas to the bottom of the roasting tin.

- Crank up the heat to 220°C/gas mark 7 for the final 30 minutes.

- When the cooking time is up, test the chicken for doneness by giving her a prick in the leg.

- Remove the chicken and chipolatas from the tin and place them on a plate suitable for carving. Put a sheet of foil over the chicken to keep her warm.

- Now for the gravy, which is the best part of any chicken dinner.

- Tilt the tin and gather the juice at one end. The fat will naturally float to the top. Spoon off as much as seems appropriate, leaving a little to absorb the flour.

- Place the tin over a medium/low heat.

- Sprinkle 1 tbs of flour into the tin and mix it with the remaining fat and juices.

- Slowly pour in around 400ml chicken stock and simmer, scraping up the crunchy bits from the bottom of the roasting tin.

- Taste and season.

  TOP TIPS: Traditional Roast Chicken is delicious with bread sauce (be lazy and buy the packet variety), mashed potatoes (essential for shoving peas into), roast potatoes, frozen peas, chipolatas, bacon, and brussels sprouts.

Chris's Parmesan Chicken

Serves 4
⌘ **£3**

3 chicken breasts
4 tbs grated Parmesan
1 tbs olive oil
35g butter, room temp
1 x 120g pot pesto sauce
1 x 142ml pot cream
300g linguine

- Grate the Parmesan onto a plate.

- Smear the breasts with a thin layer of butter as though you were applying sun tan lotion.

- Season the chicken, then dip into the Parmesan, making certain the cheese adheres to the breasts.

- Place the olive oil and remaining butter in a frying pan and set over medium heat. When the butter has melted add the breasts and cook for 6 minutes per side.

- Do not cook over too high a heat or the cheese will burn: take it easy.

- When the breasts are cooked slice them into 2cm pieces and arrange on a pile of pesto pasta.

- To make pesto cream simply mix one pot/jar of ready-made pesto with an equal amount of cream.

- Add this mixture to 300g cooked pasta.

Beef

I am strongly in favour of all people, especially growing ones, eating meat. Don't be frightened off by BSE scares. Be brave, stay buff and get stuck in.

TOP TIPS:

- Always buy british

- Keep wrapped in greaseproof paper as opposed to cling film and store in the fridge.

- Make a note of the sell-by date. It's normally safe to go a day or two over if you have kept the meat properly stored.

- Buy meat that has a decent amount of fat 'marbling' as this adds flavour.

- Salt your beef only just before cooking.

- Let beef rest for 5 to 10 minutes after cooking.

- Beef is best with:
  - Red wine or beer
  - Blue cheese
  - Onions
  - Garlic
  - Peppers
  - Mushrooms
  - Tomatoes
  - Potatoes
  - Kidneys
  - Soy sauce
  - Worcestershire sauce
  - Mustard
  - Horseradish
  - Ginger
  - Parmesan
  - Anchovies
  - Leeks

Heavenly Hamburgers

I have grown up on a routine diet of Friday night hamburgers in one form or another and I don't think you can beat a really well made hamburger for cost effective beef consumption. However, be sure to buy high quality minced steak.

Add any of these ingredients to the mince before forming into burger mode:

>Worcestershire sauce
>Soy sauce
>Tabasco sauce
>Mustard
>Onion
>Garlic
>Coriander
>Black or green olives
>Jalapeno Peppers
>Capers
>Curly parsley

These make great hamburger toppings:

>Bacon
>Sautéed mushrooms
>Sautéed onions
>Cheddar cheese
>Blue cheese
>Feta cheese
>Tomatoes
>Relish
>Mustard
>Ketchup
>Avocado
>Soured cream
>Salsa

Southwestern Burgers

Serves 4

⌘ £2

1 tbs vegetable oil
500g minced beef
12 black olives, pitted & chopped
1 tsp Tabasco sauce or chilli powder
1 tbs Dijon mustard
1/2 cup pickled Jalapeno peppers, finely chopped
4 slices of Cheddar cheese

* Place the mince in a bowl with all the other ingredients apart from the cheese and oil. Season well, then mix together thoroughly.

* Shape the mince into 4 equally sized burgers, about 4cm thick.

* Heat the vegetable oil in a frying pan and cook the burgers over medium to highish heat for 4 minutes per side. Do not cover the pan. During the last 2 minutes of cooking lay some thinly sliced cheddar cheese on top of each burger.

* Let your burgers rest for 3 minutes before eating.

   TOP TIP: Serve the with a generous dollop of soured cream and salsa.

Chilli Con Carne

Serves 4
⌘ **£2**

500g mince or shin beef
1 x 400g tin chopped tomatoes
1 x 400g tin kidney beans
1 onion, chopped
1 green pepper, chopped
2 tbs veg oil
2 cloves garlic, finely chopped
1/2 tsp cayenne pepper
1 tsp cumin
2 tbs chilli powder
500ml stock

- Pour the oil into a large saucepan over medium to low heat.

- Add the onion, pepper and garlic and gently sweat for 5 minutes.

- If you are using shin beef, cut it into 4cm pieces. Add the beef and cook over medium to high heat until browned all over. Add the spices and some salt and continue to cook for 1 minute.

- Add the tinned tomatoes and the vegetable stock.

- Turn the burner to its lowest setting and simmer for 1 to 1 1/2 hours.

- Add the drained kidney beans and cook a further 10 minutes.

- The meat should be tender and the chilli thickened to a consistency that suits you. Serve topped with soured cream and a bit of grated cheese and a green salad on the side.

Top Tips: Chilli is a great party food. It improves with age so you can make it a few days ahead of time. You can pad it out with more beans in case of unforeseen gatecrashers. If you have a deep freeze, consider brewing up a double batch.

Sloppy Joe

Serves 4
⌘ £1

2 tbs vegetable oil
1 onion, chopped
1 green pepper, chopped
500g minced beef
150ml ketchup
1 tbs vinegar
1 tbs brown sugar*
2 tsps Tabasco sauce
70ml chicken stock
4 buns

- Place the oil and chopped vegetables in a medium saucepan or frying pan and sweat for 5 minutes.

- Add the mince and cook until all the meat has gone brown. Season.

- Throw in the remaining ingredients, cover and simmer away for 15 to 20 minutes or until the sauce has thickened and you just can't wait any longer.

- Serve the Sloppy Joe oozing out of a burger bun.

  TOP TIPS: * Don't panic if you only have white sugar. Just use $1/2$ tbs instead of 1 tbs brown.

  This can be made ahead of time and left in the fridge for a few days (say 4 max).

  You can also freeze Sloppy Joe, so consider making double and freezing half.

Beef and Beer Stew

Serves 4
⌘ £2

1 kilo shin beef
2 tbs vegetable oil
2 tbs flour
1 x 440ml can of beer or ale
400ml chicken stock
2 cloves garlic, chopped
2 onions, chopped
150g small button mushrooms, whole

- Pour half the oil into a large saucepan and place over fairly high heat.

- Add the meat in 2 batches, browning and seasoning.

- When you have browned both batches of beef remove to a plate.

- Add another slosh of oil to the saucepan, add the onion and garlic and gently cook for 5 minutes over a low temperature.

- Return the meat to the pan and sprinkle with flour. Give it a good stir to coat the meat then pour in the beer and stock.

- Bring the stew to a simmer and put a lid on it. Turn the heat to its lowest setting and forget about it for at least an hour. Having said that, try to check that the stew isn't boiling and sticking to the bottom of the pan.

- After an hour add the mushrooms, whole. Cook for another 30 minutes.

- Season to taste and serve with mashed potatoes and a green salad. This stew improves with age making it a great leftover.

Top Tip: Supermarkets tend to sell stewing steak as opposed to shin beef. Try to buy shin from a butcher – it is much more tender and delicious, not to mention cheaper!

Cottage Pie

Serves 4
£2

500g minced beef
1 tbs vegetable oil
1 x 400 tin tomatoes, chopped
200ml chicken stock
1 large onion, chopped
1 tbs Worcestershire sauce
A good squirt of ketchup
1 tbs flour
1 recipe Marvellous Mash
60g or $^{1}/_{2}$ cup Cheddar cheese, grated

- Pre-heat oven to 200°C/gas mark 6.

- Pour the oil into a largish saucepan and place over medium heat.

- Add the onion and gently sweat for 5 minutes. Chuck in the mince and cook until no longer pink. Season with salt and pepper.

- Sprinkle the flour over the meat and stir to incorporate.

- Add the rest of the ingredients apart from the mash and cheese.

- Cover, and let simmer over the lowest setting for 20 to 30 minutes.

- Meanwhile, make some mashed potatoes, and grate the cheese.

- Decant the meat into a baking dish (20cm ish) and top with the mashed potatoes. Scatter the cheese over the top. The pie can be kept at this stage for a few days before eating, if stored in the refrigerator once cool.

- Put the pie in the oven for around 30 minutes. If the top does not go brown of its own accord put it under the grill for a minute or two.

Marinated Rump Steak

Serves 4
⌘ **£2**

600 to 700g rump steak, 2cm thick
2 cloves garlic, sliced
2 tbs vegetable oil
70ml Worcestershire sauce
40ml red wine

- Mix the Worcestershire sauce, wine, oil and garlic together.

- Stuff your steak into a freezer bag and pour in the marinade. Secure the top and leave to marinate for an hour or more while you pop round to the pub.

- Place a frying pan over medium/high heat. Wipe a thin film of oil over the bottom.

- When the pan looks hot throw in the steak and cook for 2 to 3 minutes each side. The cooking time will depend on your personal taste and the thickness of the steak. Test a corner for desired doneness.

- Remove the steak from the pan and place it on a warm plate to relax.

- Meanwhile pour the remaining marinade into the frying pan and simmer, scraping up any bits.

- With a sharp knife cut the steak into thin slices. Arrange the slices on a mound of Cheese Baked Potato (p.70), or Marvellous Mash (p.72) with added cheese and/or grain mustard. This is not only delicious but bulks out the steak.

- Pour the cooked marinade around the meat.

I know this is supposed to be a book of cheap eats, but hey, everyone has a week when the loan comes through. Rump is the cheapest of all steaks and with a bit of ingenious carving you can make a little go a long way. Treat yourself.

Ravishing Rumps

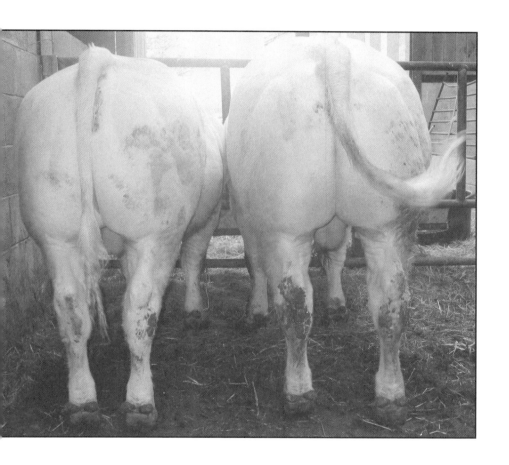

Thai Rump Steak

Serves 4

⌘ £3

600g rump steak, 2cm thick
2 cloves garlic, sliced
2 tbs ginger, finely chopped
100ml soy sauce
50ml white wine, optional
1 tbs sugar
Bunch of fresh coriander, chopped
Juice of 1 lime
1 x 250g packet fine Oriental egg noodles
1 tsp dried chilli

- Mix the soy sauce, wine, garlic, sugar and 1 tbs ginger in a jug.

- Stuff the steak into a plastic freezer bag and pour in the marinade. Secure the top, shake and leave to marinate for at least an hour.

- Wipe half the vegetable oil into a frying pan over a vicious heat.

- When the frying pan is good and hot, throw in the steak. Cook for 2 minutes per side. It will be rare, but have faith. Cook less if thinner.

- Put the steak on a plate and leave to rest. Remove the pan from heat and pour in the marinade. The pan should still be hot enough for the marinade to come to a simmer. Set to one side.

- Following manufacturers' instructions, boil up a batch of fine Chinese noodles in stock (instead of water) with a pinch of red chilli and the remaining veg oil.

- Meanwhile, slice the beef very thinly. Squeeze the lime juice over the steak and leave to 'cook' while you transfer the noodles, drained, to a deepish dish. Pour the cooked marinade over the noodles.

- Lay the slices of steak on top of the noodles and scatter the remaining ginger and chopped coriander all around.

Another spoiling recipe, but still cheaper than a take-away pizza.

Pig

Pork is my all time favourite meat. Swine have a way of turning themselves into the most delicious array of culinary delights; bacon, ham, chops, crackling, salami, sausages. What more could you ask from an animal? Pork would definitely be my Desert Island meat. There is no doubt about it.

TOP TIPS:

* For health reasons, pork must be cooked until its juices run clear, not pink. However, improvements in storage and hygiene have ensured there are fewer chances of contracting trichinosis.

* Vacuum-packed bacon and gammon last for ages unopened in the fridge.

* Once opened, eat the gammon and bacon within 5 or 6 days, if refrigerated.

* Most supermarkets sell vacuum-packed gammon joints. Occasionally they are made up of processed pork leg. They are perfectly acceptable but they tend to require longer cooking. Always read the soaking and cooking instructions on the label.

* Sausages are ideal for freezing. Try separating and freezing them as pairs.

* For really great crackling pack loads of salt onto the skin before cooking.

* Pancetta is basically smoked bacon in its Italian incarnation. I love its fattiness and smoky, cured flavour. Pancetta is the Rolls Royce of the bacon world, but like the Rolls, comes with a price tag to match. You can count on paying approximately 50% more for Pancetta than its English counterpart. I rationalize paying extra by convincing myself I need less of the full flavoured Italian variety.

* If you are roasting pork do make certain the skin has been scored. By this I mean cut into thin strips so that the skin can transform itself into delicious crackling during the cooking process.

Barbecued Spare Ribs

Serves 4
£1

1 kilo rack of pork ribs
125ml ketchup
25ml Worcestershire sauce
25ml soy sauce
1 tbs brown sugar (or $^{1}/_{2}$ tbs white sugar)
1 tbs vinegar

- Pre-heat the oven to 190°C/gas mark 5.

- Mix all the ingredients (except the ribs) in a measuring jug.

- Place the ribs in a roasting tin and pour the sauce over them. Cover with foil and place in the oven.

- Cook for 1 to 1$^{1}/_{2}$ hours then remove the foil. Mix the accumulated meat juice and sauce together in the roasting tin. Flip the ribs over and baste them with the sauce.

- Return the roasting tin to the oven, uncovered, and continue cooking for another half hour. Give the ribs one more basting after 15 minutes if you can be bothered.

- Serve with jacket potatoes that you have been cooking in the oven at the same time.

  TOP TIPS: It is really essential to buy a rack of quality joined up ribs from the butcher. Some supermarkets sell ribs that are unjoined up and altogether inferior. Use these at your own risk... you've been warned!

  You can use this barbecue sauce on chicken legs or thighs as well. The technique is the same but the cooking time is less. Bake chicken legs or thighs for 15 minutes covered, then another 15 minutes uncovered.

Crispy Pork Belly

Serves 4
£1

1 kilo belly pork, skin scored
1 tbs fennel seeds
Sea salt, loads
1 tbs vegetable oil

* Pre-heat oven to 180°C/gas mark 4.

* Make certain that the skin is scored (cut) or you will not have crackling.

* Now the fun begins. Take a fork and stab it into the pork repeatedly. This allows the fat to drain off during cooking, and allows you to let off steam.

* Shove the fennel seeds into the pork wherever you see a gap waiting to be filled.

* Rub a tiny amount of oil into the skin then pack the salt on.

* Place the pork in the oven and forget about it for at least 2 to 3 hours.

* Remove the crackling and break into pieces. The pork should be easy as pie to carve, deliciously succulent and melting in the mouth.

* Serve with lots of refreshing green or white cabbage. This will offset the richness of the meat.

Top Tips: To make a light gravy: remove the pork to a serving plate. Pour off any excess fat (you might want to leave in about 1 tsp fat for flavour). Place the roasting tin over a low heat on the top burner. Add a shot of white wine and simmer, scraping up all of the yummy bits from the bottom of the tin. After 1 or 2 minutes, add some vegetable water & lemon juice to taste.

Gammon

Delicious on its own, and a key player in many other recipes, gammon will play an important role in your survival. To save energy, put a gammon in the oven while you're cooking something else.

If you buy a gammon from the butcher, ask his advice on soaking. Supermarket gammon normally has cooking and soaking instructions printed on the label. Most supermarkets sell vacuum-packed gammon joints, smoked or unsmoked. They last for weeks in their hermetic sealing. Try to keep one in the fridge at all times. Take note. Basically, there are two simple ways of cooking gammon:

Roast Gammon

£2

1 1/2 kilo gammon
2 tbs mustard
2 tbs brown sugar

- Pre-heat oven to 180°C/gas mark 4.

- Wrap the gammon in foil and cook for 30 minutes per 500g, plus another 30 minutes uncovered. A 1 1/2 kilo gammon should take 2 hours.

- If you feel ambitious, release the gammon from the foil 30 minutes short of its cooking time. Remove the skin and smear some mustard and brown sugar over the fat. Return to the oven and continue to cook, uncovered, for the final 30 minutes.

Boiled Gammon

£2 per serving

TOP TIP: Although initially sceptical, the children and I love Nigella Lawson's recipe for ham simmered in cola. The cola really does give the ham a sweet spiky flavour. I generally use a cheap brand.

Place the gammon in a saucepan just large enough to hold it comfortably. Pour in enough cola to cover and place a lid over the top. Simmer the meat for 30 minutes per 500g. You can finish the gammon off in the oven (say the last 20 minutes) in the same way you would for the roast gammon above.

Slow Roast Shoulder of Lamb

Serves 4
£2

1 x 1 kilo shoulder of lamb, boned and rolled
Handful of springs of fresh rosemary
2 cloves garlic, sliced
4 tbs olive oil

- Pre-heat oven to 160°C/gas mark 3.

- Arrange for the lamb to arrive boned and bound.

- Slice the garlic and shove into any yielding gaps in the joint. Do the same with the rosemary. Season the lamb with liberal amounts of salt and pepper.

- Slosh some olive oil into a roasting tin and place over medium/high heat.

- Brown the lamb all over, say around a minute per surface in the tin. When you have finished with the sealing (browning), take the lamb out and wrap it, loosely, in foil.

- Rinse the roasting tin of its excess oil and put the lamb in its wrapping back in. Place in the oven and cook for 2 to 2½ hours.

- Once cooked, open the foil and carefully remove the lamb to a serving plate that you've had the foresight to warm.

- Pour the resultant juice into a saucepan and taste. You may wish to add a little water, wine, a dollop of redcurrant jelly or maybe a sprinkling of flour to thicken and make it into a nice sauce.

- There should be no need to really carve the lamb. It will pull apart in a Peking Duckish sort of way.

  Top Tip: To offset the richness of the lamb, serve with mash and a clean veg like courgettes.

Sweet Things

Chocolate Chip Cookies

200g plain flour
1 tsp bicarbonate of soda
$^1/_2$ tsp salt
150g butter
100g brown sugar
100g white sugar
1 egg
1 or 2 x 100g packet chocolate chips

- Pre-heat oven to 190°C/gas mark 5.

- Sieve the flour, bicarb and salt into a bowl.

- In another bowl, mix the butter and sugars into a smooth cream. Add the egg to the butter mixture and stir. Add the dry bits to the buttery ones. Mix thoroughly and add the chocolate chips.

- Place walnut sized blobs of the mixture on a greased baking sheet or a roasting tin.

- Allow space for the cookies to roam. Bake for 10 to 12 minutes.

Meringues

4 egg whites
200g caster sugar

- Pre-heat oven to 140°C/gas mark 1.

- Put the egg whites into a squeaky-clean mixing bowl and whisk until they appear cloud-like and billowing. Add 50g of the sugar and whisk for a minute. Add the remaining sugar and whisk until the sugar is incorporated.

- Pull a sheet of greaseproof paper over the roasting tin and blob the meringue mix on in large serving spoon-sized mounds.

- Cook in a very cool oven for 1 to $1^1/_2$ hours.

    Top Tips: Meringues are the perfect use for leftover egg whites. You can just leave them to hang out in a cooling oven while you get on with something else. Try breaking the cooked meringues into pieces and mixing them with yoghurt or cream and fruit. Passion is my fave fruit.

Brownies

Serves as many as you like

125g butter
6 tbs cocoa powder
2 eggs
250g sugar
6 tbs self-raising flour
1 x 100g bag chocolate chips

- Pre-heat oven to 180°C/gas mark 4.

- Grease a baking dish measuring around 20 x 25cm or so.

- Mix the eggs and sugar in a small bowl.

- Melt the butter with the cocoa. When the butter is melted add to the sugar mixture and gently stir. Sieve the flour over the top and fold in. Do not over mix. Add the chocolate chips and pour into the baking dish. Cook for 35 minutes. The brownies will be squishy in the centre but will firm up with cooling.

  TOP TIP: To enhance the brownies add 1 tbs chopped herb of choice to the batter, before baking.

Vodka Jelly

1 packet of your favourite flavoured jelly
Equal parts water and vodka

- Make the jelly according to the instructions on the packet, substituting vodka for half the water.

Baked Bananas

Serves 4
£1

3 bananas
100g brown sugar
80ml water
Juice of 1 lemon
1 tbs chopped stem ginger (optional)

- Pre-heat oven to 190°C/gas mark 5.

- Mix the water, ginger and sugar in a small saucepan and simmer until the sugar has dissolved.

- Peel the bananas, cut them in half lengthways and place them in an ovenproof dish. Squeeze the lemon all over the bananas and pour on the sugar water. Cover with foil and bake for 30 minutes. Serve warm with ice cream, cream or yoghurt.

Top Tip: The lemon juice stops the bananas going brown if they're prepared in advance.

Ice Cream

There's no point pretending you'll be making your own ice cream. However, you can make adjustments to the sort you buy. Try mixing chopped stem ginger, crunched up Crunchy, demolished Dime Bar or mashed Maltesers with plain old vanilla ice cream:

As for toppings, try sliced bananas, runny honey and peanuts, muesli, fresh fruit or:

Fudge Sauce

Serves 6
⌘

175ml double cream
3 tbs Golden Syrup
1 cup sugar
100g chocolate, broken into pieces
30g butter
1 tsp vanilla essence

- Place the sugar, syrup and cream in a small saucepan over medium/low heat and cook until the sugar dissolves. Add the chocolate and simmer until it melts and the sauce thickens.

- Remove from the heat and whisk in the butter. Serve warm over ice-cream.

Butterscotch Sauce

Serves 6
⌘

142ml double cream
50g butter
75g brown sugar

- Place all the ingredients in a small saucepan and simmer for 5 minutes, or until the sauce has thickened. Serve warm or at room temp over ice-cream.

Fran's Favourite Banana Bread Muffins

Makes 8 muffins
V £1

250g cups plain flour
2¹/₂ tsp baking powder
80g butter or margerine
150g sugar
2 large eggs
2 enormous ripe bananas
16 x 'Super Cook' American muffin cases

- Pre-heat oven to 180°C/gas mark 4.

- Blend the fat until creamy, then add the sugar and blend again. Throw in the eggs and mix thoroughly.

- Sift the flour and baking powder into a bowl. Add to the butter mixture and then stir.

- Mash the bananas with a fork or potato masher. Whatever. Fold into the batter.

- Fill muffin cases (doubled-up so they keep their shape) to slightly over half. Place them on a baking sheet or roasting tin and bake for 20 minutes.

TOP TIPS: These make the ultimate all-in-one brain-blasting breakfast on the run. Make muffins even healthier by adding another banana or a tablespoon of wheat germ and/or bran. If you like nuts, throw a handful of walnuts into the batter.

Store muffins in a plastic container or biscuit tin. They'll stay fresh for 3 to 4 days depending on the banana content.

You can easily freeze muffins. and mic them for 30 seconds before dashing out the door. Freeze in a plastic bag.

Bread and Butter Pudding

Serves 4
£1

8 to 10 slices French baguette, 2cm thick
70g butter
200ml milk
42ml double cream
100g sugar
3 eggs, lightly beaten

- Pre-heat oven to 180°C/gas mark 4.

- Melt the butter in a saucepan. Dip the bread in the butter and lay in an ovenproof dish, around 20cm x 25cm ideally.

- Warm the milk and cream in the old butter pan

- Lightly beat the eggs and sugar in a bowl, then add to the milk mixture.

- Pour the eggy milk through a sieve onto the bread. Scatter a few raisins on top if you fancy and some caster sugar to golden things up a bit.

- Cook for 30 minutes.

  TOP TIP: This recipe is excellent for using up stale bread.

Off The Wall Recipes

Confessions of a Tin Opener . . . .

Tomato, Bean and Pasta Soup

Serves 4
⌘ £1

2 x 400g tins cannellini or butter beans beans, drained
1 x 400g tin plum tomatoes
2 cloves garlic, sliced
1 tbs olive oil
800ml chicken or veg stock
150g soup pasta such as small macaroni

- Slice the garlic then place in a medium saucepan with the olive oil.

- Sweat over medium/low heat for a minute then add the tomatoes, chopped down a little in their tin, and stock. Bring to the boil then add one tin of beans.

- Mash the beans from the second tin with the back of a fork. Add to the soup along with the pasta.

- Simmer according to the instructions on the pasta.

Cannellini Bean Soup

Serves 2
⌘ £1

2 tbs olive oil
1 clove garlic, chopped
2 x 400g cannellini beans, drained
400ml chicken or veg stock

- Put the oil in a small/medium saucepan and add the chopped garlic. Sweat for 1 to 2 minutes. Don't brown the garlic.

- Add the stock and one tin of beans. Mash the other tin of beans, then add these. Simmer for 10 minutes.

Pasta with Tuna, Capers and Black Olives

Serves 4
⌘ £1

400g pasta
1 x 200g tin tuna
2 tbs capers
Handful of black olives
4 to 5 tbs olive oil

- Cook the pasta al dente and place in a large serving bowl.

- Drain and flake the tuna. Add to the pasta with the olives and capers.

- Give the whole lot a drowning (well, not quite) in olive oil.

Pasta with Anchovies and Butter

Serves 2
⌘ £1

200g pasta
1 x 50g tin anchovies
60g butter, room temperature

- Cook the pasta in oiled and salted boiling water. Drain and transfer to a large serving bowl.

- Drain the anchovies and rinse, while still in their tin, with water. Put them on a plate and cut into quarters.

- Put the butter on the plate with the fish and mash all together using the back of a fork so you end up with a fishy paste.

- Add the anchovy mixture to the pasta and stir thoroughly. Freshly ground black pepper is delicious with this dish.

TOP TIP: For really fishy pasta add 1 x 200g tin of tuna.

Pasta with Onions

Serves 2
⌘ £1

1 onion
1 tbs balsamic vinegar, optional
3 tbs olive oil
200g pasta

- Cut the onion in half and slice as thinly as you possibly can.

- Sauté the onions in a saucepan with 1 tbs of olive oil. Allow the onions to become slightly burnished as this gives them more flavour. The principle is, the longer they cook, the sweeter they become.

- Add the vinegar after 10 minutes and let it 'cook off' (evaporate).

- Cook the pasta according to the instructions on the packet.

- Serve the pasta with the remaining olive oil and top with the onion.

Pasta with Olive Oil, Garlic and Chilli

Serves 4
⌘ £1

5 tbs olive oil
3 cloves garlic, finely chopped
2 tsp dried chilli, or as hot as you can take it
400g pasta

- Boil a large pot of water. Add a splash of olive oil and some salt.

- Place oil, garlic, and chilli in a small saucepan and gently warm on low heat. Be careful not to brown the garlic.

- When the pasta is al dente, drain and place in a warmed serving bowl or back into the cooking pot. Drizzle with the garlicky oil and serve with plenty of fresh parmesan.

Even More Store Cupboard Ideas:

Pasta with Pesto Sauce
Pasta with Butter and Crushed Pepper
Pasta with Sun Dried Tomatoes, Olives and Garlic

Lentils with Olives

Serves 2
⌘

150g Puy lentils
400ml stock
Handful of black olives
2 tbs olive oil
Pinch of rosemary
Pinch of thyme

- Cook the lentils in the stock and herbs for 35 minutes or until tender. Add more stock if necessary.

- Put the lentils in a serving dish and anoint with olive oil. Add the olives and season well.

TOP TIP: Feta or goat's cheese pad this out a treat.

Chickpea Curry

Serves 2
⌘

1 x 425 tin chickpeas
1 potato, diced
1 onion, chopped
1 clove garlic, chopped
1 tsp each cumin, chilli powder and chopped ginger
250ml chicken or veg stock
1 tbs vegetable oil

- Gently sweat the onion and garlic in the oil for 5 minutes in a large saucepan.

- Add the spices and cook a further minute.

- Peel and dice the potato into cubes roughly twice the size of the chickpeas. Add the potatoes, chickpeas and stock to the saucepan and simmer for 10 minutes, or until the potatoes are tender. Season, then serve.

Cannellini Beans with Tuna

Serves 4

2 x 400g tins canellini beans
2 x 200g tins tuna fish
3 tbs olive oil
Juice of 1 lemon or 1 tbs vinegar

* Open the tins of beans and drain.

* Repeat the opening and draining process with the tuna.

* Place the contents of all the tins in an eye-catching serving dish.

* Mix the oil and lemon juice, season to taste, and drizzle all around.

    TOP TIP: If you have any red or spring onions to hand, thinly slice and drape them around in a decorative fashion.

Mediterranean Chickpea Salad

Serves 3 or 4

2 x 400g tins chickpeas
6 sun dried tomatoes
Handful of olives
1/2 onion, finely chopped
3 tbs olive oil
2 tsp vinegar

- Drain the peas and place in a bowl. Chop the tomatoes into an acceptable size and add to the peas along with the onion and olives.

- Mix the olive oil and vinegar together in a mug and season. Pour the dressing over the chickpeas and give them and good stir.

  TOP TIP: Chopped red pepper really livens things up. Feta or goats cheese are both delicious in this salad. Fresh mint is yummy strewn in amongst the peas.

Hassle free Hummous

1 x 400 tin chickpeas
1 clove garlic, mashed
1 tsp dried chilli
1 tsp ground cumin
Juice of one lemon
3 tbs olive oil

- Drain the peas into a large plastic bowl and reduce them to a pulp with a potato masher or fork.

- Add all the remaining ingredients, mix well and season to taste.

  TOP TIP: Eat with toast, pitta bread or nachos.

Planning Menus

Sample Weekly Menu Planners

I know this sounds unbelievably nerdy but give me a chance to explain. These weekly menu planners have an important role to play in your civilized survival and will be of enormous help. I promise. They set out to achieve the following:

- Use the oven to cook two dishes at once. Saving money.
- Use leftover food in other recipes throughout the week. Saving time.
- Use the same ingredients in different guises. Saving shopping.

With a little forward planning you can minimize your shopping, save time and create the backbone of your week's cooking in one lazy Sunday morning.

Buy the papers, make yourself a cup of coffee, set your oven and do the following:

Roast 2 x 1¹/₂ kilo chickens *
Roast 1 x 1¹/₂ kilo gammon *

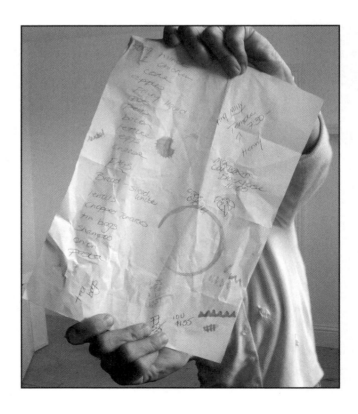

Weekly Menu Planner 1

Sunday

Chicken with bacon
Chipolatas
Mashed potatoes **
Frozen peas **
Gravy

Monday

Frittata with gammon and cheese **

Tuesday

Caesar salad with cold chicken

Wednesday

Southwestern Burgers **

Thursday

Pasta with gammon, peas and cream

Friday

Cottage Pie

Saturday

Jacket Potatoes with gammon cubes and cheese

* Use leftovers of the gammon and chicken in other recipes.

** Make or buy larger quantities of the following for use in other dishes: use cheese again with pasta and potatoes; buy masses of mince for both burgers and pie; get plenty of peas for lunch and pasta; make a mountain of mash for both Sunday lunch and cottage pie.

Weekly Menu Planner 2

Sunday

Fast Roast Chicken *
Along with a Sunday lunch of:
Crispy Pork Belly
Marvellous Mash **
Cabbage **

Monday

Minestrone Soup
Cold chicken

Tuesday

Smoked Haddock with Mustard Mash
Spinach **

Wednesday

Pasta with Sausage and Spinach **

Thursday

Crispy Jacket Potatoes
Roast Gammon *
Carrots

Friday

Sausage and Lentils

Saturday

Cheese Baked Potatoes with Gammon Slices

* Use leftovers for other recipes

** Make or buy larger quantities and use in other recipes, for example: make extra mash, use it for the Smoked Haddock with Mustard Mash. Buy enough sausage for the Pasta and Lentil recipes. Use leftover gammon in the potato bake. Use spinach again in pasta. Buy plenty of cabbage and use leftovers in the Minestrone.

Shopping Lists for the sample menus

Menu 1

Meat
2 chickens
1 x 2 kilo gammon
8 chipolata sausages
1 kilo minced beef
8 to 10 slices streaky bacon

Salad & Veg
3 Cos lettuces (bought throughout the week)
2 kilos mashing potatoes
2 onions
4 baking potatoes

Groceries
1 tin chopped tomatoes
1 jar Jalapeno peppers
1 jar Salsa
1 x 50g tin anchovies
Olive oil
Black olives
Mayonnaise

Bakery
1 sliced loaf

Dairy
100g Parmesan cheese
600g Cheddar cheese
1 x 142g pot soured cream
2 x 250g butter
12 eggs
1 x 284g pot double cream

Freezer
1 x 680g bag frozen peas

Cost up to about £50

Menu 2

Meat
1 chicken
1 x 1 kilo pork belly
60g bacon
$1^{1}/_{2}$ kilo gammon
8 sausages

Salad & Veg
3 kilos potatoes
2 cabbages
1 swede
3 parsnips
4 onions
Bunch of celery
2 x 250g bags spinach
200g courgettes
1 bag of carrots
1 x garlic bulb

Groceries
2 tins tomatoes
1x 500g pasta of choice
1 bag of lentils

Dairy
1 x 250g butter
100g Gruyère cheese
150g Cheddar cheese
1 litre milk

Fishmonger
600g smoked haddock

Cost up to about £40

These lists are based on 4 people eating each dish.

Breakfast

I'm now going to sound like everyone's mother and bang on about breakfast being the most important meal of the day. It's sad but true. Try to think of it as a form of early morning brain-blasting. Get out of bed 10 minutes earlier and get it down yer.

TOP TIPS:

- Store a loaf of sliced bread in the deep freeze. You can hack out a slice and toast it from frozen. Freeze muffins and bagels as well.

- Always have Long Life milk in store.

- Keep your cereal well wrapped inside its box. It stays crunchier that way. Check out Value-pack muesli which is super-fibrous and better value than most cereals.

- Keep a bowl of fruit on hand. Bananas are particularly good for breakfast.

- Keep your jam in the fridge if possible. This prevents mould appearing.

- There is little to beat a warm bowl of porridge on a dark winter morning. It sets you up for the day. Instant oats only take minutes to prepare and are much cheaper to buy than, say, a box of Cornflakes.

- Try to avoid buying your breakfast at a café or Starbucks once at work/college. A cappuccino and croissant breakfast is incredibly expensive.

Breakfast on the Run

Having established the importance of a healthy breakfast, there are ways of making it a brief encounter…

Orange Smoothie

$^{1}/_{2}$ **cup OJ**
$^{1}/_{2}$ **cup plain yoghurt**
1 ripe banana
1 tbs honey
Squeeze of lemon

• Blend all the above until smooth. You can tote it along with you in an empty plastic water bottle.

TOP TIP: This will only work if you have a blender of sorts, but it's the perfect way to take in your daily fruit. You can use any fruit to make smoothies.

Bagels

An ideal breakfast for a busy day. They take minimal preparation, travel well, and can be eaten for lunch as well as breakfast.

Eat Bagels:
• Toasted
• With cream cheese
• With cream cheese and jam
• With peanut butter and banana
• Raisin bagel with butter and cinnamon sugar *

* To make cinnamon sugar, place 1 part ground cinnamon to 2 parts sugar in a bowl or ramekin, and mix together. Also excellent on toast.

Bacon Butty

• Place 2 or 3 rashers of bacon on a double sheet of kitchen roll on a plate in the microwave. Cover with another sheet of kitchen roll and cook on full power for 3 minutes while you clean your teeth. Place the bacon on a buttered bap, and dash.

Index